IBM Cognos Insight

Take a deep dive into IBM Cognos Insight and learn how this personal analytics tool can be integrated with other IBM Business Analytics products

Sanjeev Datta

[PACKT] enterprise

professional expertise distilled

PUBLISHING

BIRMINGHAM - MUMBAI

IBM Cognos Insight

Copyright © 2012 Packt Publishing

All rights reserved. No part of this book may be reproduced, stored in a retrieval system, or transmitted in any form or by any means, without the prior written permission of the publisher, except in the case of brief quotations embedded in critical articles or reviews.

Every effort has been made in the preparation of this book to ensure the accuracy of the information presented. However, the information contained in this book is sold without warranty, either express or implied. Neither the author, nor Packt Publishing, and its dealers and distributors will be held liable for any damages caused or alleged to be caused directly or indirectly by this book.

Packt Publishing has endeavored to provide trademark information about all of the companies and products mentioned in this book by the appropriate use of capitals. However, Packt Publishing cannot guarantee the accuracy of this information.

First published: November 2012

Production Reference: 1071112

Published by Packt Publishing Ltd.
Livery Place
35 Livery Street
Birmingham B3 2PB, UK.

ISBN 978-1-84968-846-8

www.packtpub.com

Cover Image by Faiz Fattohi (faizfattohi@gmail.com)

Credits

<table>
<tr><td>Author
Sanjeev Datta</td><td>Project Coordinator
Priya Sharma</td></tr>
<tr><td>Reviewer
Kirk Wiseman</td><td>Proofreader
Maria Gould</td></tr>
<tr><td>Acquisition Editor
James Keane</td><td>Indexer
Hemangini Bari</td></tr>
<tr><td>Commissioning Editor
Meeta Rajani</td><td>Production Coordinator
Melwyn D'sa</td></tr>
<tr><td>Technical Editors
Kirti Pujari
Pooja Pande</td><td>Cover Work
Melwyn D'sa</td></tr>
</table>

About the Author

Sanjeev Datta is a seasoned Consultant, passionate text and video blogger, and Business Analytics enthusiast. As Practice Director at PerformanceG2, Inc., he works extensively with executives and decision-makers across finance, manufacturing, retail, and pharmaceuticals as a trusted advisor in corporate performance management, building client relationships and managing Business Analytics implementations.

Sanjeev's work as a strong Project Manager, Pre-sales and Post-sales Consultant, trainer, and mentor has led to many successful implementations. While at Merador, LLC, Sanjeev worked as a Consultant/Architect building solutions for global organizations.

Previous to that, Sanjeev was a Cognos Developer/Consultant while at Softpath Systems, LLC and lead successful Cognos BI solutions and developed Cognos BI training material for numerous clients.

He is certified in numerous IBM products and is an IBM Technical Specialist and IBM Sales Mastery Professional.

Sanjeev has a degree in Computer Science from Mumbai University and a degree in Interdisciplinary Studies from The University of Texas.

Connect with Sanjeev on LinkedIn or Twitter: @1dsanjeev

About PerformanceG2, Inc:

PerformanceG2 is a full-service IBM Premier Partner and Performance Management Consultancy that helps organizations achieve breakthrough performance. PerformanceG2 offers a comprehensive package of performance management solutions including business analytics tools, Business Intelligence Roadmap services, custom onsite Cognos training, online Cognos training, financial performance management solutions, Cognos support, staffing services, consulting services, and more—all delivered by a team of experienced consultants and award-winning trainers.

Acknowledgement

Every piece of work has people and experiences that help in giving it shape and taking it to the finish line, and I hope this acknowledgement lets you know how much I truly appreciate your efforts.

Personally, I would like to thank my wife and co-worker, Dhrity. Your kindness and support have made this possible. Thanks for listening to my ideas in the middle of the night. To our beautiful daughter, Lyzah, your smile makes every day seem to go by easily. Thanks to my mother for her prayers throughout and my father who once told me: *Never complain about working too hard, because there is always someone who is working harder for lesser*. Thanks to my sister for the competitive encouragement. Thank you all for the great experiences!

Professionally, I would like to thank PerformanceG2, Inc. Candace Taylor for being the best marketing professional I've come across. Kirk Wiseman: my good friend, career guide, and guru. Gary Frings and Michael Bloch for helping me grow and for your leadership skills. You all make the best team to work for!

Thanks to Packt Publishing, specifically Meeta Rajani and Priya Sharma for your guidance and professionalism throughout this process. To Kerry George of Pearson PLC (UK), for believing in the idea of this book. Thank you to Mr. Hemang Desai of Softpath Systems, LLC for your call that one November afternoon that kicked off my career.

Lastly, thanks to the IBM Business Analytics team for making this and other great products.

I've thoroughly enjoyed writing this book. I hope you enjoy reading it and gain much knowledge from it.

About the Reviewer

Kirk Wiseman is the Vice President of Services for PerformanceG2, an IBM Premier partner that specializes in Business Analytics. Kirk has over 15 years experience in the Information Technology industry with an emphasis in Business Analytics, specifically with Cognos where he spent over eight years of his career supporting the North and South American Cognos user base as a trainer, consultant and architect. Kirk came to PerformanceG2 from Merador where he was Director of Training Services. Prior to Merador, Kirk was a trainer and consultant at Cognos Corporation where he was recognized with awards including North American trainer of the year and Eclipse Outstanding Performance. In addition, Kirk was a Program Director at ITI, a private post-graduate school located throughout Canada. Kirk holds a Bachelor of Science degree from Memorial University of Newfoundland and a post graduate diploma in Applied Information Technology from ITI.

Kirk contributes Business Analytics videos to YouTube on a regular basis that can be viewed at `http://www.youtube.com/PerformanceG2` and he blogs at `http://www.performanceg2.com/blog`.

You can contact Kirk at `kirk.wiseman@performanceg2.com`.

I would like to thank Sanjeev for putting together a primer for Cognos Insight and Packt for giving me the opportunity to review. I hope my feedback proved helpful. Much love and thanks for my wife, Mireille and our three children, Aiden, Zachary, and Kaelyn.

www.PacktPub.com

Support files, eBooks, discount offers and more

You might want to visit `www.PacktPub.com` for support files and downloads related to your book.

Did you know that Packt offers eBook versions of every book published, with PDF and ePub files available? You can upgrade to the eBook version at `www.PacktPub.com` and as a print book customer, you are entitled to a discount on the eBook copy. Get in touch with us at `service@packtpub.com` for more details.

At `www.PacktPub.com`, you can also read a collection of free technical articles, sign up for a range of free newsletters and receive exclusive discounts and offers on Packt books and eBooks.

`http://PacktLib.PacktPub.com`

Do you need instant solutions to your IT questions? PacktLib is Packt's online digital book library. Here, you can access, read and search across Packt's entire library of books.

Why Subscribe?

- Fully searchable across every book published by Packt
- Copy and paste, print and bookmark content
- On demand and accessible via web browser

Free Access for Packt account holders

If you have an account with Packt at `www.PacktPub.com`, you can use this to access PacktLib today and view nine entirely free books. Simply use your login credentials for immediate access.

Instant Updates on New Packt Books

Get notified! Find out when new books are published by following `@PacktEnterprise` on Twitter, or the *Packt Enterprise* Facebook page.

Table of Contents

Chapter 3: Usability of IBM Cognos Insight — 43

Chapter 4: Strategic Decision Making Using IBM Cognos Insight — 91

Preface

Fast analytics is the new addiction! As decision making yearns to get faster, easier, and more accurate by the decade, technology giants such as IBM continue to invest billions of dollars to bring their strategy and business visions to reality. This book encompasses those billion dollar ideas and innovations into a new product from IBM's Business Analytics division.

IBM Cognos Insight is the new analytics software targeted to improve decision making at all levels. It starts with the basic concepts of business intelligence and advanced analytics but has the ability to expand from medium to enterprise levels by collaborating and sharing data analysis seamlessly. The in-memory computing improves querying performance and the options to connect to different data sources including IBM Cognos suite of products establishes this as a robust and flexible application.

As part of the IBM Cognos family of products, Cognos Insight is regarded as the personal analytics, "desktop-residing" application that provides rich dashboard style reports in minutes. The simplicity and intuitiveness of this product minimizes the learning curve and empowers the end user by making them proactive and independent in their efforts to analyze data. As the end users build their analysis, they have the ability to deploy to larger audiences seamlessly or share their analysis offline and sync up their contributions once back in connected online mode.

With the in-memory engine, corporations can leverage the write-back capabilities to build budgets, plans, and forecasts. This alternate scenario building technology helps analysts and decision makers in formulating better business cases for industry domains ranging across finance to risk management, procurement to information technology, and so on.

The ability to collaborate and share data analysis with larger work groups across the organization is accomplished using the high-fidelity, centralized, and administratively-governed publishing mechanism which increases productivity and adds immediate business value.

IBM Cognos Insight's features and functionalities lower the total cost of ownership (TCO) hugely due to reduced software and associated hardware license costs, a self-service approach to a simple yet powerful product that minimizes the learning curve and maximizes usability, and enterprise deployment capabilities, thereby generating a high return on investment (ROI).

This book provides new and existing users of business analytics with details about IBM Cognos Insight from an implementation, installation, and usability approach. IBM's vision, leadership, and new product, Cognos Insight, were the inspiration behind writing this book which also helped achieve my personal goal of being a published author.

What this book covers

Chapter 1, The New-age Analytics and IBM Cognos Insight introduces the concept of business analytics and the technologies such as Business Intelligence, Performance Management, Predictive Analytics, and Risk Management that have fused together to form the core of Analytics. This chapter then introduces IBM Cognos Insight as the new in-memory, desktop application from IBM and focuses on the path of a successful Business Analytics implementation.

Chapter 2, Installing IBM Cognos Insight installs IBM Cognos Insight and sets up the application to be a collaborative tool with IBM TM1 and IBM Cognos Business Intelligence.

Chapter 3, Usability of IBM Cognos Insight is meant to showcase the features and functionalities of the product with explanations of its benefits and uses. At the end of the chapter, IBM Cognos Insight workspaces should be easy to build.

Chapter 4, Strategic Decision Making Using IBM Cognos Insight talks about the business cases of using IBM Cognos Insight in the real world and how to leverage the information in *Chapter 3, Usability of IBM Cognos Insight* to build workspaces in Cognos Insight for finance, sales, marketing, and advertising groups.

Chapter 5, Enterprise Collaboration demonstrates the deployment of IBM Cognos Insight workspaces into IBM Cognos BI and TM1 products. This chapter will demonstrate the power and seamless publish mechanism that takes the desktop built workspaces into enterprise environments.

References provides the sources that will be quite valuable to you.

What you need for this book

A desire for "fast-analytics-now" is the key requirement for this book. The product speaks for itself and the book shows new and existing users all the aspects of the product. Having a computer around with the minimum product requirements mentioned in *Chapter 2, Installing IBM Cognos Insight* will help in learning the features in *Chapter 3, Usability of IBM Cognos Insight* and finally building the workspaces in *Chapter 4, Strategic Decision Making Using IBM Cognos Insight*. Having access to Cognos or TM1 environments will benefit those readers looking to publish their workspaces. Nonetheless, the book gives readers all the information required to work on a day to day basis with the IBM Cognos Insight.

Who this book is for

This book is for anyone and everyone looking to build personal analytics. With a simple desktop installation, the product is ready to go in minutes and builds dashboards in seconds. This product is for those in and out of the corporate world who are looking for immediate answers. This product and the book bring value to any organization by beginning with small to medium analyses and deploying them to enterprise-grade environments. The menu driven creation of dashboard style analysis and the ability to share them creates an organization-wide waterfall effect by going from the desktop to server with minimal to no coding required.

Conventions

In this book, you will find a number of styles of text that distinguish between different kinds of information. Here are some examples of these styles, and an explanation of their meaning

New terms and **important words** are shown in bold. Words that you see on the screen, in menus or dialog boxes for example, appear in the text like this: "Click on **Explore** in the title bar to see the **Explore Pane**".

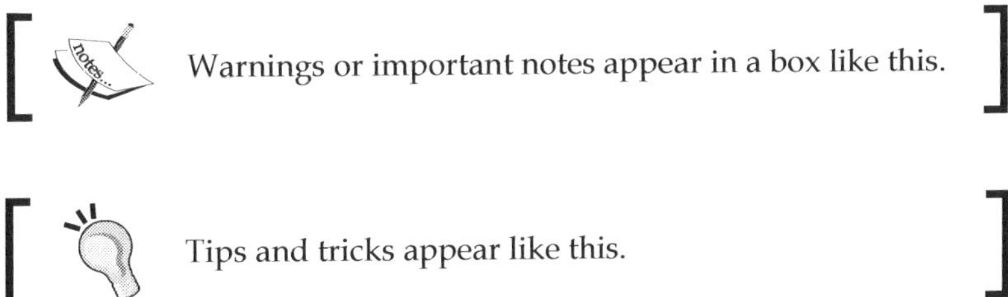

Reader feedback

Feedback from our readers is always welcome. Let us know what you think about this book—what you liked or may have disliked. Reader feedback is important for us to develop titles that you really get the most out of.

To send us general feedback, simply send an e-mail to `feedback@packtpub.com`, and mention the book title through the subject of your message.

If there is a topic that you have expertise in and you are interested in either writing or contributing to a book, see our author guide on `www.packtpub.com/authors`.

Customer support

Now that you are the proud owner of a Packt book, we have a number of things to help you to get the most from your purchase.

Downloading the example code

You can download the example code files for all Packt books you have purchased from your account at `http://www.packtpub.com`. If you purchased this book elsewhere, you can visit `http://www.packtpub.com/support` and register to have the files e-mailed directly to you.

Errata

Although we have taken every care to ensure the accuracy of our content, mistakes do happen. If you find a mistake in one of our books—maybe a mistake in the text or the code—we would be grateful if you would report this to us. By doing so, you can save other readers from frustration and help us improve subsequent versions of this book. If you find any errata, please report them by visiting `http://www.packtpub.com/support`, selecting your book, clicking on the **errata submission form** link, and entering the details of your errata. Once your errata are verified, your submission will be accepted and the errata will be uploaded to our website, or added to any list of existing errata, under the Errata section of that title.

Piracy

Piracy of copyright material on the Internet is an ongoing problem across all media. At Packt, we take the protection of our copyright and licenses very seriously. If you come across any illegal copies of our works, in any form, on the Internet, please provide us with the location address or website name immediately so that we can pursue a remedy.

Please contact us at `copyright@packtpub.com` with a link to the suspected pirated material.

We appreciate your help in protecting our authors, and our ability to bring you valuable content.

Questions

You can contact us at `questions@packtpub.com` if you are having a problem with any aspect of the book, and we will do our best to address it.

1
The New-age Analytics and IBM Cognos Insight

Business decision making relies on data analysis. Over the time, the analytical proficiency has improved with technological advancements in software and the supporting hardware. To satisfy the growing demands of quality data analysis, organizations such as IBM are constantly investing in better hardware and software applications that not only meet the business demands but also tackle the current needs such as exponential data growth, predicting outcomes from historical data trends, managing risks real time, and applying smarter analytical capabilities over structured and unstructured data.

IBM Cognos Insight is one of IBM's newest innovations surrounding smarter analytics. A software product installed on desktops yet runs in memory, and builds fast analytical cubes to answer the four broad questions—*what, when, why,* and *how*. IBM Cognos Insight answers these questions by working with numerous types of data to provide deeper insights to help make better business decisions. Coupled with genius algorithms and rich visual, descriptive and textual outputs, this new product has the capabilities to start at a desktop level and launch into an enterprise-wide Business Analytics solution.

We use analytics in every sphere of life, be it financial services, consumer behavioral management, healthcare management, human capital management, risk management, sales and marketing, or technology, to name a few. Business Analytics is a term that sums up the various analytical domains. It serves to improve the business performance and adds to the total business value by leveraging on raw data, and trusting the processes and software applications to provide smarter analytical capabilities.

Business Analytics is gaining more recognition in the business world than ever before. It provides management teams with a competitive advantage, business performance visibility, and high **Returns On Invested Capital (ROIC)**. In a joint MIT Sloan Management Review and IBM's **Institute for Business Value (IBV)**, the top-performing organizations use analytics five times more than the lower performers.

The following chart tracks the differences between the tendencies of the top-performing organizations versus the lower performing organizations in terms of usage of business analytics:

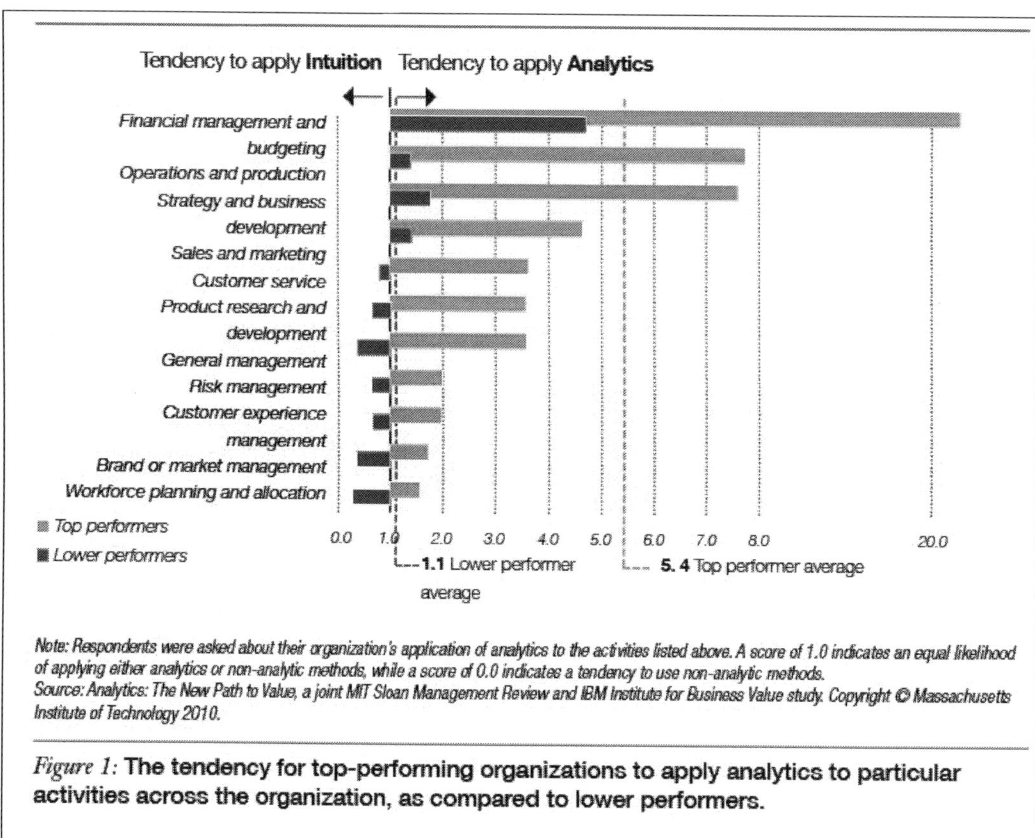

Note: Respondents were asked about their organization's application of analytics to the activities listed above. A score of 1.0 indicates an equal likelihood of applying either analytics or non-analytic methods, while a score of 0.0 indicates a tendency to use non-analytic methods.
Source: Analytics: The New Path to Value, a joint MIT Sloan Management Review and IBM Institute for Business Value study. Copyright © Massachusetts Institute of Technology 2010.

Figure 1: **The tendency for top-performing organizations to apply analytics to particular activities across the organization, as compared to lower performers.**

The graph shows that the lower performing organizations tend to use intuition when it comes to customer service, risk management, product research and development, and so on, within their organization, which might suggest improper (or no) use of business analytics at an enterprise level. Thus they have a higher probability of not making the cut of a top performing organization.

To understand Business Analytics further, it is important to understand its building blocks and take a deeper dive into its core components. The four main components that fall under the Business Analytics umbrella are shown in the following diagram:

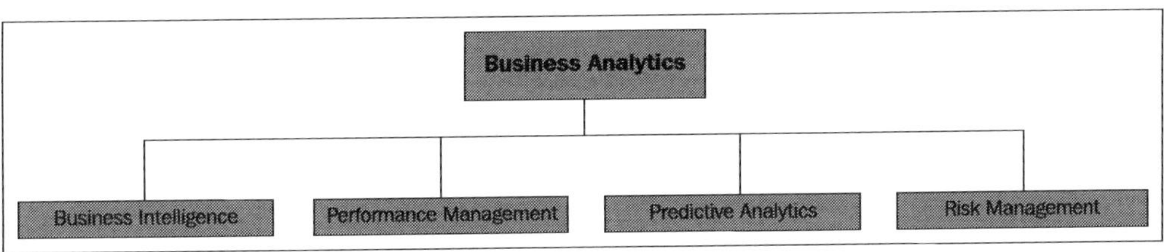

The following are the explanations for these four building blocks:

- **Business Intelligence (BI)**: This was first described by computer scientist Hans Peter Lunn of IBM in 1958 as an "intelligence system that will utilize data-processing machines for auto-abstracting and auto-encoding of documents…for creating interest profiles for each of the "action points" in an organization". The definition has changed over the years with advancements in technology which IBM today defines as: "BI helps predict, track, analyze, and present information as it relates to business performance".

- **Performance Management**: Performance Management asks scenario-based questions to organizations and their departments with the intention of improving their overall health. These *what-if* simulations are an input to gain insight and to add value to the business. Typically consisting of planning, budgeting, and forecasting solutions, performance management tends to improve the financial processes, and increases the profitability for all the organizations that invest in its processes and methodologies.

- **Predictive Analytics**: Predictive Analytics, as the name suggests, predicts the future outcomes by trending the historical values mixed with intelligent calculations and algorithms from mining, on structured and unstructured data. Statistical analysis towards various data models enable the prediction of outcomes ranging from text mining on social media to correlation analysis that link entities, for understanding the growing volumes of data better.

- **Risk Management**: Risk Management applications provide risk analysis and manage change in the regulations along with compliance procedures and governance regulations to reduce financial losses.

Analytics with IBM Cognos Insight

IBM Cognos Insight is the a new product on IBMs Business Analytics block installed on desktops and capable of supporting the five pillars of business intelligence and analytics — reporting, advanced analytics, visual dashboards, score carding, and predictive and risk analytics. The following diagrams hows the features of IBM Cognos Insight:

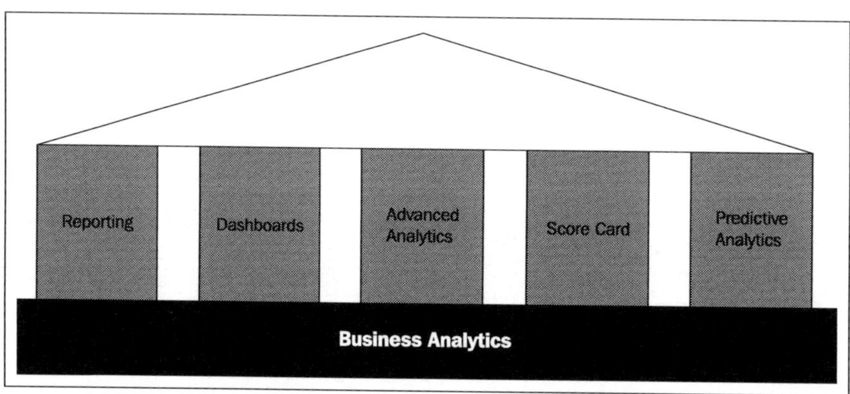

Features of IBM Cognos Insight

The simplicity of the application lies in its drag-and-drop functionality and built-in smart metadata wizard that enables importing spreadsheets and other types of databases. This desktop application is built upon the robust foundations of **IBM TM1** (formerly **Applix**), which stores the data in the memory and in multi-dimensional formats. Much like the structure of a rubix cube, data analysis is performed by analyzing multiple dimensions of the cube structure. In addition, the cube compresses and rolls up the data points into levels to form a hierarchical design that can be analyzed by drilling up and drilling down, or slicing and dicing across the multiple-dimensions for a complete analytical exploration.

From a performance stand point, IBM Cognos Insight is an in-memory application that makes for faster development and enhances analysis efforts. Coupled with its visual appeal and data exploration capabilities, it makes for a tremendously powerful reporting and dashboard application. With IBM TM1 as the underlying technology and with its write-back functionality, part of the advanced analytics provides the *what-if* scenario approach used for an alternate scenario analysis.

It also helps in spreading the data across plans, budgets, and forecasts, which the organizations are looking for to give greater financial visibility and improved business performance. Even when not connected to a server system, IBM Cognos Insight provides write-back, report authoring, dashboard designing, and scorecard developing capabilities in its offline mode, as the data resides within the application and syncs to larger deployments on demand.

IBM Cognos Insight has the ability to share authored reports and dashboards that can be distributed to larger workgroups, collaborating on the same data sets and towards similar goals. The collaborative effort is a huge plus for this self-service desktop application. As per an IBM Institute for Business Value (IBV) study in which 1700 CEO's were interviewed globally, 75 percent of the CEOs demand collaboration as a priority among its workforce. Another benefit of sharing a stand-alone data asset with larger workgroups is that is provides standardization across departments, and governance with workflow processes that have an overall effect towards improvement in performance.

All of the features mentioned here minimize the IT involvement and hand-holding for a technology application used in the business world, thereby making organizations more self-sufficient and agile.

An example case for IBM Cognos Insight

Consider an example of a situation where an organization from the retail industry heavily depends on spreadsheets as its source of data collection, analysis, and decision making. These spreadsheets contain data that is used to analyze customers' buying patterns across the various products sold by multiple channels in order to boost the sales across the company. The analysis hopes to reveal customers' buying patterns demographically, streamline sales channels, improve supply chain management, give an insight into forecast spending, and redirect budgets to advertising, marketing, and human capital management, as required.

As this analysis is going to involve multiple departments and resources working with spreadsheets, one of the challenges will be to have everyone speak in similar terms and numbers. Collaboration across departments is important for a successful analysis. Typically in such situations, multiple spreadsheets are created across resource pools and segregated either by time, product, or region (due to the technical limitations of spreadsheets) and often the analysis requires the consolidation of these spreadsheets to be able to make the educated decision. After the number-crunching, a consolidated spreadsheet showing high level summaries is sent out to executives, while the details remain on other tabs within the same spreadsheet or on altogether separate spreadsheet files. This manual procedure has a high probability of errors.

The similar data analysis process in IBM Cognos Insight would result in faster decision making by keeping the details and the summaries in a highly compressed **Online Analytical Processing (OLAP)** in-memory cube. Using the intuitive drag-and-drop functionality or the smart-metadata import wizard, the spreadsheet data now appears instantaneously (due to the in-memory analysis) in a graphical and pivot table format. Similar categorical data values, such as customer, time, product, sales channel and retail location are stored as dimension structures. All the numerical values bearing factual data such as revenue, product cost, and so on, defined as measures are stored in the OLAP cube along with the dimensions. Two or more of these dimensions and measures together form a cube view that can be sliced and diced and viewed at a summarized or a detailed level. Within each dimension, elements such as customer name, store location, revenue amount generated, and so on, are created. These can be used in calculations and trend analysis. These dimensions can be pulled out on the analysis canvas as explorer points that can be used for data filtering and sorting. Calculations, business rules and differentiator metrics can be added to the cube view to enhance the analysis.

After enhancements to the IBM Cognos Insight workspace have been saved, these workspaces or files can be e-mailed and distributed as offline analyses. Also, the users have the option to publish the workspace into the IBM Cognos Business Intelligence web portal, Cognos Connection or IBM Cognos Express, both of which are targeted to larger audiences, where this information can be shared with broader workgroups. Security layers can be included to protect sensitive data, if required. The publish-and-distribute option within IBM Cognos Insight is used for advanced analytics features and write-back functionality in larger deployments. where, the users can modify plans online or offline, and sync up to the enterprise environment on an as-and-when basis. As an example, the analyst can create *what-if* scenarios for business purposes to simulate the introduction of a new promotion price for a set of smart phones during high foot traffic times to drive up sales. Or simulating an extension of store hours during summer months to analyze the effects on overall store revenue can be created.

The following diagram shows the step-by-step process of dropping a spreadsheet into IBM Cognos Insight and viewing the dashboard and the scorecard style reports instantaneously, which can then be shared on the IBM Cognos BI web-portal or published to an IBM TM1 environment.

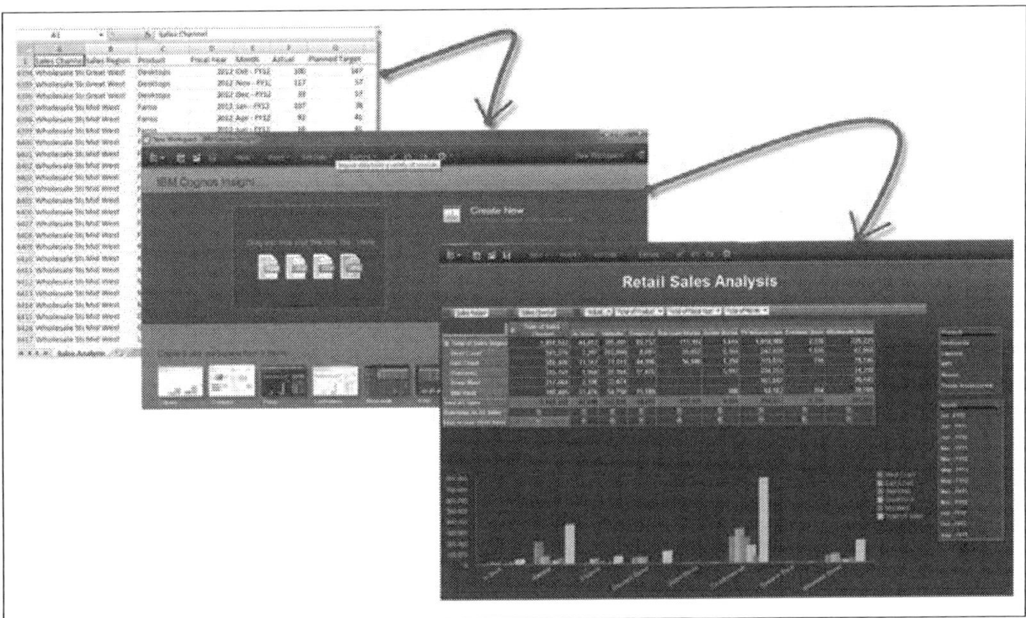

The preceding screenshot demonstrates the steps from raw data in spreadsheets being imported into IBM Cognos Insight to reveal a dashboard style report instantaneously. Additional calculations to this workspace creates scorecard type graphical variances, thus giving an overall picture through rich graphics.

The building blocks of Business Analytics

The four building blocks or components of Business Analytics comprise of Business Intelligence, Performance Management, Predictive Analytics, and Risk Management. Built to perform and deliver as a Business Analytics software, IBM Cognos Insight can answer the business queries from each of these components.

Business Intelligence

Decision making that is based on large volumes of data can be a daunting task and using data intelligently, and converting it into an asset to reveal answers that help decision making easier is defined as Business Intelligence. Transactional and operational reporting, scorecards, and analysis together form the basis of Business Intelligence.

IBM Cognos Insight provides the basis of business intelligence through its features. Leveraging on the cube design fundamentals of dimensions and measure for analysis, creating business reports and scorecards displaying variances are the core features and benefits that enable Business Intelligence capabilities. The drag-and-drop functionality or the smart-metadata import wizard provides value in reducing time consuming processes such as requirements gathering and depending on IT to build reports. Users of IBM Cognos Insight can benefit from publishing workspaces as starting points for reports, which can be further customized and formatted in IBM Cognos BI or IBM Cognos Express environments, thereby creating Cognos Report Studio reports for each published workspace. This saves tremendous amounts of time in building simple to complex BI reports.

Performance Management

Executives rely on data to answer questions, so they can make the difficult decisions and/or strategic moves that will define the fate of their organization. Questions, such as the following, can be answered intelligently using Performance Management methodologies, which take an organization's performance to the next level and ahead of the competitors:

- How can our revenue grow faster?

- How and why are our competitors out-performing us?

- Where can we trim the expenses for a lean structure?

- When should we see a profit on a new product?

- How can we structure bonus payouts to maximize employee retention?

Performance Management can be applied to any part of the Business world as it improves the decision making capabilities and gives insight into the day-to-day operations, strategic moves and future investments, streamlines processes, automates procedures and so on. The write-back functionality enables simulating business scenarios that demonstrate alternative business cases that eventually lead towards the right decision making for any organization.

From a performance management perspective geared towards the financial health of an enterprise, **Financial Performance Management (FPM)** plays a key role where CFOs are constantly engaged in maintaining a balance between reducing costs and increasing profitability from the customers and product bands. Other **Key Performance Indicators (KPIs)** of financial growth are as follows:

- Gross profit
- Net profit
- Interest rates
- Variable costs
- GL expenses
- Labor, material, and production costs
- Marketing and advertising costs
- Operating variances
- Assets and liabilities
- Net cash flow

Using IBM Cognos Insight, these metrics can be graphically, comparatively, or numerically displayed, and vital financial reports such as profit and loss statements, balance sheets, and income and cash flow statements to name a few, can be authored to give deeper financial insight into the functioning of the organization. The simulation of alternate business cases using write-back technology is often used for creating budgets, plans, and forecasts.

IBM Cognos Insight is used as a Performance Management application and in areas such as Financial Performance Management (FPM) to increase revenue growth, lean operating expenses, shorten financial close processes and improving corporate planning, budgeting, and forecasting processes in many organizations.

Predictive Analytics

Prior to the year 2007, before the boom of social networking, if a product was shipped out we didn't receive a direct feedback from the consumer until after the product was a sell-out or a high percentage of returned items were received.

Five years later, it is a different situation as vast amount of data is collected, analyzed, and business decisions are made faster. These vast amounts of data can be used to measure patterns and be able to predict the outcomes based on past trends. IBM Cognos Insight connects to these predictive databases such as IBM SPSS to quickly analyze the current market scenarios so that businesses can act faster on customer feedback.

IBM Cognos Insight has the capability to connect to predictive data to analyze future outcomes. An example of a Customer Relationship Management case is a call center. Cognos Insight uses the predictive data to read the customers intentions before connecting live with the customer, thereby giving higher risk callers faster attention over other satisfied customers. Not only does this improve customer service but reduces the risk of losing the customer by providing IBM Cognos Insight dashboards, based on the customers' behavioral patterns and past positive preferences.

Risk Management

A Risk Management case where IBM Cognos Insight can provide high value in predictive modeling is when it collaborates with IBM SPSS to predict natural disasters from past patterns before they arise. An alert system can flag disaster management and first-response entities to prepare the insurance companies better, thereby reducing the risk before the disaster arrives. Cognos Insight can act as a desktop application for various field experts who can input live data into their dashboard design workspaces and publish them into a centralized Cognos BI environment. This collaborative effort between experts on the field and other organizations using IBM Cognos Insight and Cognos BI provides fast decision making capabilities. This in turn can minimize the stress on the government and the financial institutions with reduced insurance damage payouts.

In Other cases where Business Analytics using IBM Cognos Insight, IBM Cognos BI and IBM SPSS serves industries is to ensure higher customer satisfaction, better sales pipelines, greater product yields, better order fulfillments, reduced overall risks, and avoiding bottlenecks in complex supply chains.

The power of Analytics today is applied in and outside of the business world. IBM Cognos Insight can leverage spreadsheets, IBM Cognos BI content, and other database systems (relation, statistical, and so on) through ODBC connections, to build faster analytics. Cognos Insight can act as a provider of data that might not exist in the organization's main database systems.

With all the data in the world today, 90 percent of which has been created over the last two years alone, Analytics is going from the business world into the world of sports. **Sports Analytics** is the term used to define what global sport associations and groups are doing with predictive analytics (using statistics and mathematics) by tapping into years of historical data to spot trends and predict the outcomes of games before they begin and well before they end.

One such example recently has been the 2012 Wimbledon Championship, where IBM's Business Analytics team set up IBM SlamTracker. A web product that displays data in visual dashboard styles to display in real-time, player statistics using key metrics such as number of aces, the percentage of wins on the first serve, the percentage of wins, percentage on the second serve, receiving points won, break points conversions, net approaches, and other such parameters. SlamTracker analyzes 39 million data points available over the last seven years of all the Grand Slams for each player to come up with a player pattern in real time.

Using Analytics in sports is taking place in other sports leagues as well such as **National Basketball Association (NBA)**, **National Hockey League (NHL)**, **National Football League (NFL)**, Soccer World Cups, and the Olympic games.

Using analytics successfully

Over the past few years, there have been huge improvements in the technology and processes of gathering the data. Using Business Analytics and applications such as IBM Cognos Insight we can now analyze and accurately measure anything and everything. This leads to the question: Are we using Analytics successfully?

The following high-level recommendations should be used as a guidance for organizations that are either attempting a Business Analytics implementation for the first time or for those who are already involved with Business Analytics, both working towards a successful implementation:

1. The first step is to *prioritize* the targets that will produce intelligent analytics from the available trustworthy data. Choosing this target wisely and thoughtfully has an impact on the success rate of the implementation. Usually, these are high value targets that need problem solving and/or quick wins to justify the need and/or investment towards a Business Analytics solution.

2. Avoid the areas with a potential for probable budget cuts and/or involving corporate cultural and political battles that are considered to be the major factors leading to an implementation pitfall. Improve your chances by asking the question—where will we achieve maximum business value?

3. Selecting the appropriate product to deliver the technology is the key for success—a product that is suitable for all the skill levels and that can be supported by the organization's infrastructure. IBM Cognos Insight is one such product where the learning curve is minimal; thanks to its ease of use and vast features. The analysis produced by using IBM Cognos Insight can then be shared by publishing to an enterprise-level solution such as IBM Cognos BI, IBM Cognos Express, or IBM TM1. This product reduces dependencies on IT departments in terms of personnel and IT resources due to the small learning curve, easy setup, intuitive look, feel, and vast features. The sharing and collaborating capabilities eliminate the need for multiple silos of spreadsheets, one of the reasons why organizations want to move towards a more structured and regulated Enterprise Analytics approach.

4. Lastly, organize a governing body such as a **Analytics Competency Center (ACC)** or **Analytics Center of Excellence (ACE)** that has the primary responsibility to do the following:

    - Provide the leadership and build the team
    - Plan and manage the Business Analytics vision and strategy (BA Roadmap)
    - Act as a governing body maintaining standardization at the Enterprise level
    - Develop, test, and deliver Business Analytic solutions
    - Document all the processes and procedures, both functional and technical
    - Train and support end users of Business Analytics
    - Find ways to increase the **Return on Investment (ROI)**
    - Integrate Business Analytics into newer technologies such as mobile and cloud computing

The goals of a mature, enterprise-wide Analytics solution is when any employee within the organization, be it an analyst to an executive, or a member of the management team, can have their business-related questions answered in real time or near real time. These answers should also be able to predict the unknown and prepare for the unforeseen circumstances better. With the success of a Business Analytics solution and realized ROI, a question that should be asked is—are the solutions robust and flexible enough to expand regionally/globally? Also, can it sustain a merger or acquisition with minimal consolidation efforts?

If the Business Analytics solution provides the confidence in all of the above, the final question should be — can the Business Analytics solution be provided as a service to the organizations' suppliers and customers?

Summary

As analytics advances with technological improvements and innovations with tools such as IBM Cognos Insight, decision making capabilities will only get faster and more accurate. IBM Cognos Insight provides the starting point in analytics with offline capabilities for business users, with the option of taking their development efforts to an enterprise level so as to share and collaborate with teams within their organization. Being able to build dashboards in minutes with powerful analytical capabilities makes IBM Cognos Insight an application for all.

The next chapter will show a step-by-step installation procedure of IBM Cognos Insight. The readers will be able to then build their own analytical solutions to answer business-related questions and get deeper insights.

2

Installing IBM Cognos Insight

IBM Cognos Insight has a simple, wizard-driven installation procedure. This desktop application can be used in a stand-alone mode for personal analytics or can be used as a collaborative application, sharing its workspaces into IBM Cognos Business Intelligence or IBM Cognos Express environments. With an in-memory analytical (OLAP) engine under the covers, IBM Cognos Insight can extend its collaborative functionality to other IBM Business Analytics domains such as performance management (IBM TM1), predictive analytics, and mobile devices.

Before planning an IBM Cognos Insight installation, careful attention should be given to the supported environments such as the operating system, server environments, and data sources and their connectivity options, so as to successfully install and use all the features of the application.

System requirements for installing IBM Cognos Insight

Here is a list of environments that will support IBM Cognos Insight.

Processor and memory

The following should be considered as the minimum system requirements for using IBM Cognos Insight. A faster processor, additional memory, and disk space will contribute to a better performance; specifically when dealing with larger volumes of data and complex design.

- Processor: 1500 Megahertz (MHz) processor or higher
- Memory: 2 gigabytes (GB) or higher
- Hard disk: 500 megabytes (MB)
- Display: 1024 x 768 or higher resolution

Operating systems

IBM Cognos Insight can be installed on the following operating systems:

- Microsoft Windows XP Professional SP3 32-bit
- Microsoft Windows Vista SP2
- Microsoft Windows 7 Professional 32-bit/64-bit

The following are the system requirements for users installing and configuring IBM Cognos Insight for versions other than the Personal Edition and Standard Editions. The versions that require server information, data sources, and query builder information are:

- IBM Cognos Insight Provision install for IBM Cognos Business Intelligence
- IBM Cognos Insight Provision Install for IBM Cognos Express
- IBM Cognos Insight Provision Install for IBM TM1

Cognos Server environments

Server Environments	Share	Publish
IBM Cognos BI 10.1.1 64-bit Installation on UNIX	Compatible	Not Supported
IBM Cognos BI 10.1.1 32-bit/64-bit Installation on Windows	Compatible	Not Supported
IBM Cognos BI 10.2	Active	Active
IBM Cognos TM1 10.1	N/A	Compatible
IBM Cognos TM1 10.1.0.1	N/A	Compatible
IBM Cognos TM1 10.1.1	N/A	Active

High - Fidelity publish is not supported in IBM Cognos 10.1.1

Data sources

The following Data Sources are supported by IBM Cognos Insight 10.2.

- ODBC
- IBM Cognos BI 10.1.1 List Reports (Report Studio)
- IBM Cognos BI 10.2 List Reports (Report Studio)
- IBM Cognos BI 10.1.1 Packages
- IBM Cognos BI 10.2 Packages

- IBM Cognos TM1 10.1 Cube Views/Subsets
- IBM Cognos TM1 10.1.0.1 Cube Views/Subsets
- IBM Cognos TM1 10.1.1 Cube Views/Subsets
- Microsoft Excel 2007, 2010
- Delimited text file
- Other Data Sources via ODBC
    ◦ DB2 10.2
    ◦ DB2 9.7
    ◦ DB2 9.1, 9.5
    ◦ MS SQL 2008
    ◦ MS SQL 2005
    ◦ Oracle 11g Release 2
    ◦ Oracle 10g Release 2
    ◦ SPSS .sav

Server environments for IBM Cognos Connection installer

The following are the server environments for IBM Cognos Connection installer:

- Microsoft Windows Server 2008 R2 SP1 (Standard/Enterprise Edition) 32-bit/64-bit
- Microsoft Windows Server 2008 R2 (Standard/Enterprise Edition) 32-bit/64-bit
- Microsoft Windows Server 2008 R2 (Web/Datacenter Edition) 32-bit/64-bit
- Microsoft Windows Server 2008 SP2 (Standard) 32-bit/64-bit
- Microsoft Windows Server 2008 SP2 (Enterprise/Web/Datacenter Edition) 32-bit/64-bit
- Microsoft Windows Server 2008 (Standard/Enterprise/Web/Datacenter Edition) 32-bit/64-bit
- Microsoft Windows Vista SP2 (Cognos Connection only)
- Microsoft Windows 7 SP1 32-bit/64-bit (Cognos Connection only)
- Microsoft Windows XP Professional SP3 32-bit/64-bit
- IBM AIX 7.1 64-bit
- IBM AIX 6.1 64-bit

- HP-UX 11i v3 Itanium 64-bit
- HP-UX 11i v2 Itanium 64-bit
- Novell SUSE Linux Enterprise 11 (IBM Power)
- Novell SUSE Linux Enterprise 11 (IBM System z)
- Novell SUSE Linux Enterprise 11 64-bit Novell SUSE Linux Enterprise 10 SP3 (IBM System z)
- Novell SUSE Linux Enterprise 10 SP1 64-bit
- Red Hat Enterprise Linux AP 6.3 and above (IBM Power)
- Red Hat Enterprise Linux AP 6.3 and above 64-bit
- Red Hat Enterprise Linux AP 5.8 and above (IBM Power)
- Red Hat Enterprise Linux AP 5.8 and above 64-bit
- Red Hat Enterprise Linux ES/WS 5.8 and above 64-bit
- Red Hat Enterprise Linux AS/ES/WS AP 4.6 and above (IBM Power)
- Red Hat Enterprise Linux AP 4.6 and above 64-bit
- Red Hat Enterprise Linux AS/ES/WS 4.6 and above 64-bit
- Sun Solaris 10 (SPARC) 64-bit
- Sun Solaris 9 (SPARC) 64-bit

For an updated version of the IBM Cognos Insight supported environments, visit the IBM webpage at `http://www-01.ibm.com/support/docview.wss?uid=swg27025127`.

Available options to download Cognos Insight

IBM Cognos Insight provides multiple versions of installing, based on the user's needs and availability of other IBM products within the installing environment. Download IBM Cognos Insight from `https://www.analyticszone.com` or from the available CD/DVDs as provided.

- Personal Edition: This version of Cognos Insight can be downloaded from the IBM Insight community website at `https://www.analyticszone.com`. This is a free version with limited features.

This version allows the importing of data source files (`.xls` or `.csv` files only). The ODBC connectivity and connecting to the Cognos server for BI Reports are disabled features. This application can be used as a personal analytics solution with no sharing capabilities and this allows for analyzing and exploring data. The intention is to use this version for non-commercial, personal use and is installed with the user having administrator rights to the computer.

If you wish to upgrade to the Standard Edition, uninstall this version first and then install the Standard Edition. Keep in mind Provision type installations from Cognos BI or TM1 will overwrite this version of IBM Cognos Insight.

- Standard Edition: This version of IBM Cognos Insight is a stand-alone version with the ability to use spreadsheets (CSV and XLS) and other data sources via ODBC connections to create analyses. Like the Personal Edition, the Standard Edition also requires that the users have administrator rights on the computer where Cognos Insight will be installed. The installation files have combined 32-bit and 64-bit components that are used to install with the appropriate operating system. This version allows users to share their development efforts with other users of the same version but keep in mind that the Personal or Provisional versions will overwrite the Standard versions of Cognos Insight.

- Provision install for existing IBM Cognos BI Environments: Available for both Windows (32-bit and 64-bit) and Unix Environments, this option is useful when Cognos BI is already available in the installing environment. The advantage of this option is that it allows multiple end users to download Cognos Insight from the web portal—Cognos Connection—after the Cognos BI Administrator assigns these selected users either the Advanced Business Author or Enhanced Consumer roles. This ensures all the users are on the same version of Cognos Insight.

  This version of Cognos Insight completely integrates into the Cognos BI environment, allowing for publishing workspaces from Cognos Insight into Cognos Connection. The ability to publish dashboards, contribute to plans (write-back analysis), and sharing Cognos Insight (`.cdd`) files to Cognos connection. It uses Report Studio reports or Framework Manager packages as data sources as well, which differentiates this version from the Standard and Personal Editions.

  There are two steps involved when installing this version of Cognos Insight. The first is installing the IBM Cognos Connection Installer on the available Cognos BI servers (version 10.1.1 or higher).

The second step will allow the end user to install Cognos Insight on-demand, straight onto their desktops, from the Cognos Connection web portal.

As shown in the following screenshot, when a user logs into IBM Cognos BI's web portal Cognos Connection, a new item appears in the **My Actions** section. Once the user clicks on the highlighted portion, Cognos Insight is installed on the user's desktop. This is the provision install from Cognos BI and benefits by standardizing all the users on the same version of Cognos Insight.

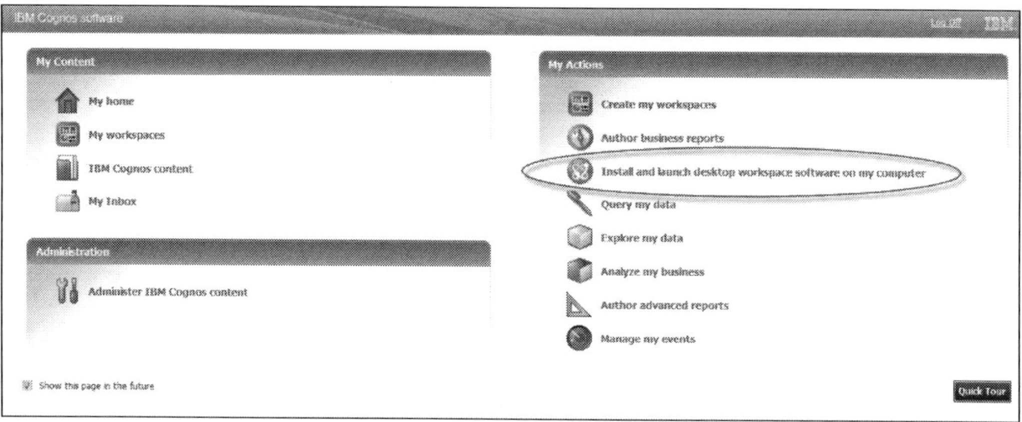

- IBM Cognos Express: IBM Cognos Insight can also be installed from Cognos Express environments either through Cognos Express Planner or Cognos Express Advisor. This provision method ensures users are on the same version of Cognos Insight and prompts users if newer versions are found on the servers where Cognos Express is installed.

- IBM TM1 10: IBM Cognos Insight can also be installed from TM1 10.1 version (and higher). This option is available in the TM1 environment for users who belong to the "Contributor" or higher role. The functionality within this option of installing Cognos Insight includes all the above features such as data analysis, exploration, sharing with other Cognos Insight users and publishing & distributing to the Cognos BI environment and TM1 environment via Performance Modeler. This Cognos Insight version features the write-back capability and business rules applications for scenario analysis and planning, similar to TM1 Environments.

When installing Cognos Insight from an existing IBM TM1 environment, users can install Cognos Insight from the TM1 application portal. As this version of Cognos Insight resides on the TM1 server, users are notified to upgrade their local versions, if the server has a newer version of Cognos Insight.

Installing IBM Cognos Insight Standard Edition

The following are the step-by-step instructions to install IBM Cognos Insight Standard Edition.

1. Once the installation file has been unzipped, double-click on the `win32` folder as shown next. If you are installing directly from a CD/DVD the `Autorun.inf` file will execute automatically to run the wizard, bypassing the next two steps.

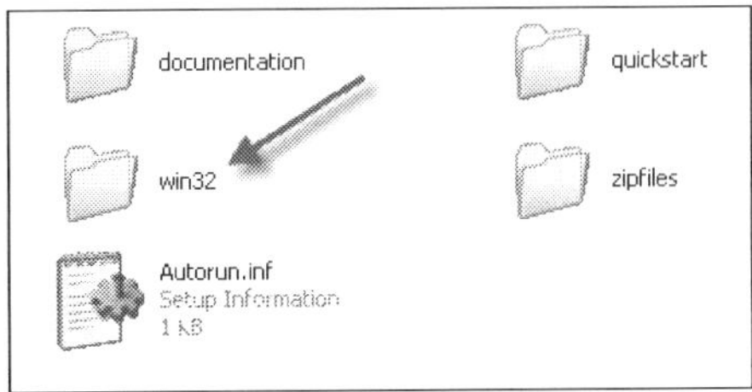

2. The following screenshot shows all the files inside the `win32` folder. When executed, the file `issetup.exe` starts the installation wizard that will help us install the product on a local computer.

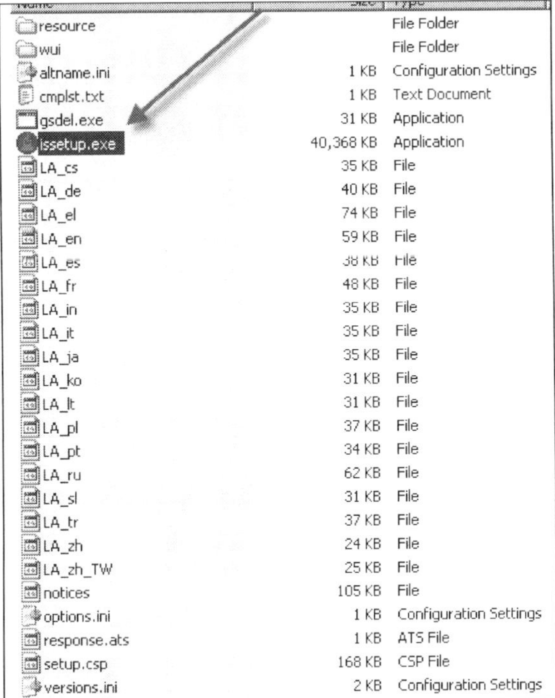

Name	Size	Type
resource		File Folder
wui		File Folder
altname.ini	1 KB	Configuration Settings
cmplst.txt	1 KB	Text Document
gsdel.exe	31 KB	Application
issetup.exe	40,368 KB	Application
LA_cs	35 KB	File
LA_de	40 KB	File
LA_el	74 KB	File
LA_en	59 KB	File
LA_es	38 KB	File
LA_fr	48 KB	File
LA_in	35 KB	File
LA_it	35 KB	File
LA_ja	35 KB	File
LA_ko	31 KB	File
LA_lt	31 KB	File
LA_pl	37 KB	File
LA_pt	34 KB	File
LA_ru	62 KB	File
LA_sl	31 KB	File
LA_tr	37 KB	File
LA_zh	24 KB	File
LA_zh_TW	25 KB	File
notices	105 KB	File
options.ini	1 KB	Configuration Settings
response.ats	1 KB	ATS File
setup.csp	168 KB	CSP File
versions.ini	2 KB	Configuration Settings

The following image shows the Install Stream program that will generate the wizard. Notice that the version on the product is **10.2**.

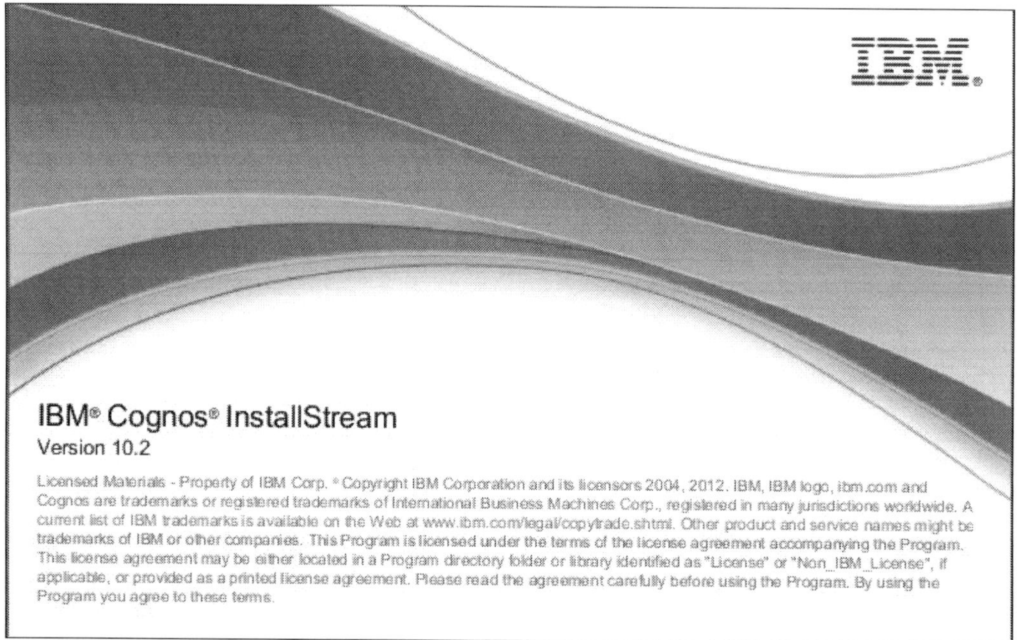

3. The following image shows the first screen in the wizard — the **Welcome** screen. **Language Selection** for the installation process and access to the installation guide is available, as seen in the following screenshot:

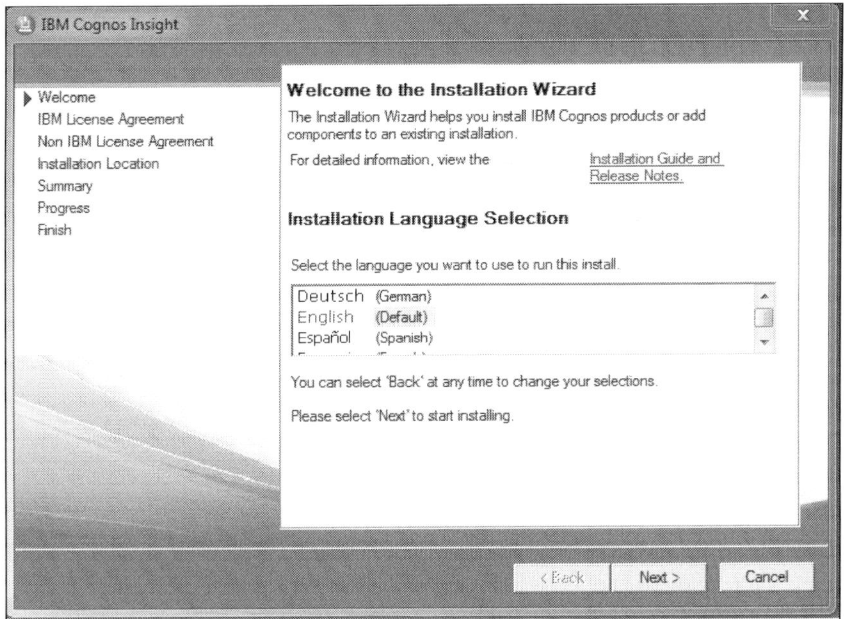

4. The following screenshot shows the **IBM License Agreement**. Read and understand the agreement and then select the **I Agree** radio option to proceed with the installation process.

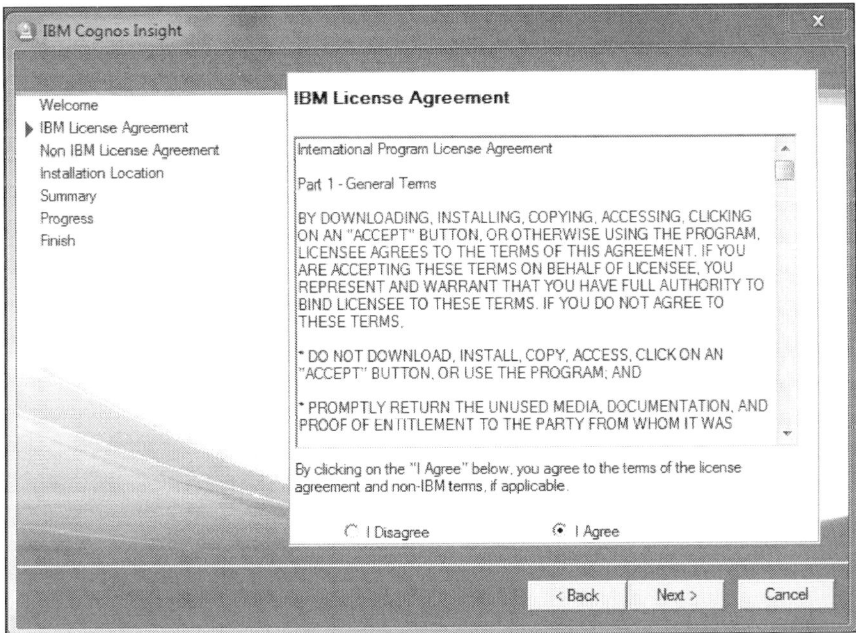

5. The next screenshot shows the location of the installer file—`CognosInsight.msi`. By default IBM Cognos Insight Installer is installed at the path `C:\Program Files\IBM\CognosInsight` for a 32-bit installation on a 32-bit Microsoft Windows system.

   If you are installing the 32-bit Cognos Insight on a 64-bit Microsoft Windows system, the default location would be `C:\Program Files(x86)\IBM\Cognos\CognosInsight/`.

For users installing IBM Cognos Insight from IBM Cognos BI, the Cognos Connection Installer is installed in the following locations:

- `C:\Program Files\IBM\Cognos\c10` folder for a 32-bit installation on a 32-bit Windows system
- `C:\Program Files\IBM\Cognos\c10` folder for a 64-bit installation on a 64-bit Windows system
- `C:\Program Files(x86)\IBM\Cognos\c10` folder for a 32-bit installation on a 64-bit Windows system

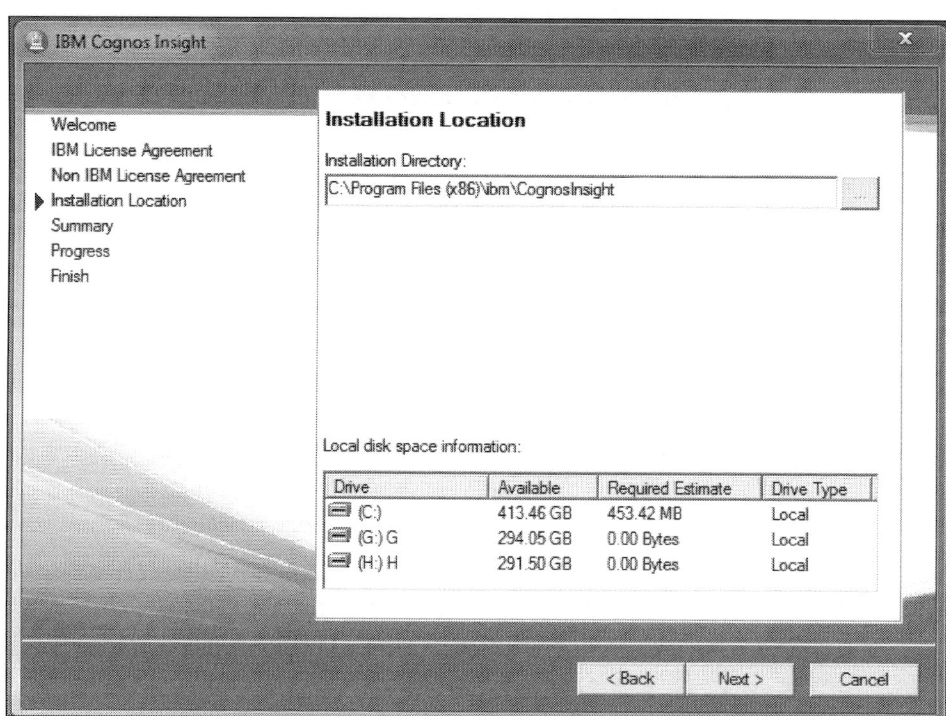

6. The following screenshot shows the **Installation Summary** of the Cognos Insight Install that is about to begin. This confirmation page shows the following:

    ° Local disk space (required and available): **Local disk space information**

    ° Installation location: **Dialog Entry Information**

    ° Installation logs location on the machine: **Summary-Error Log Location**

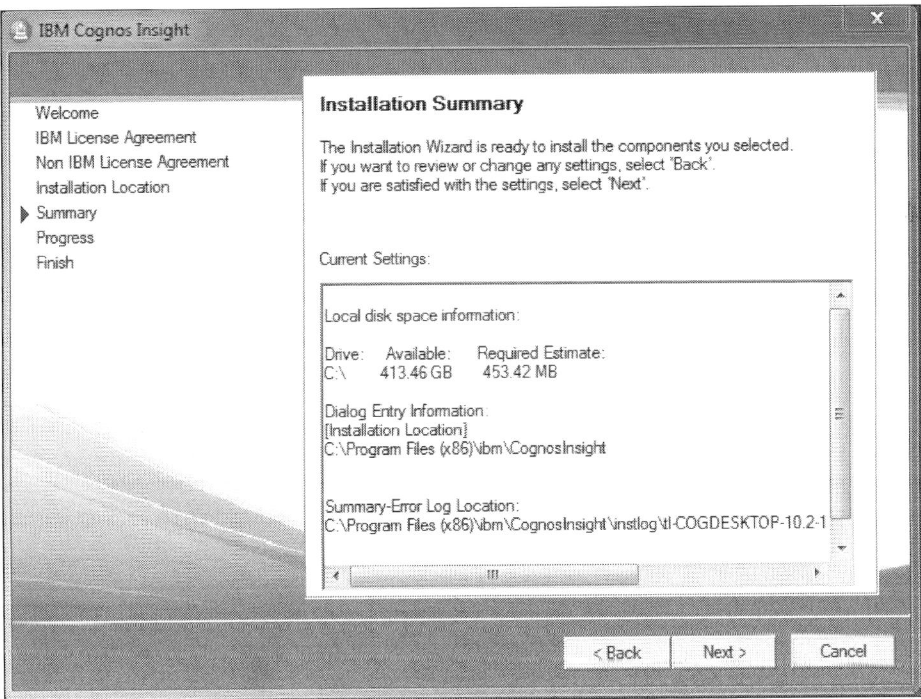

7. For confirming the installation, click on **Next.** The following screenshot shows the installation status. Once all of the 17 components are installed, the setup is completed successfully:

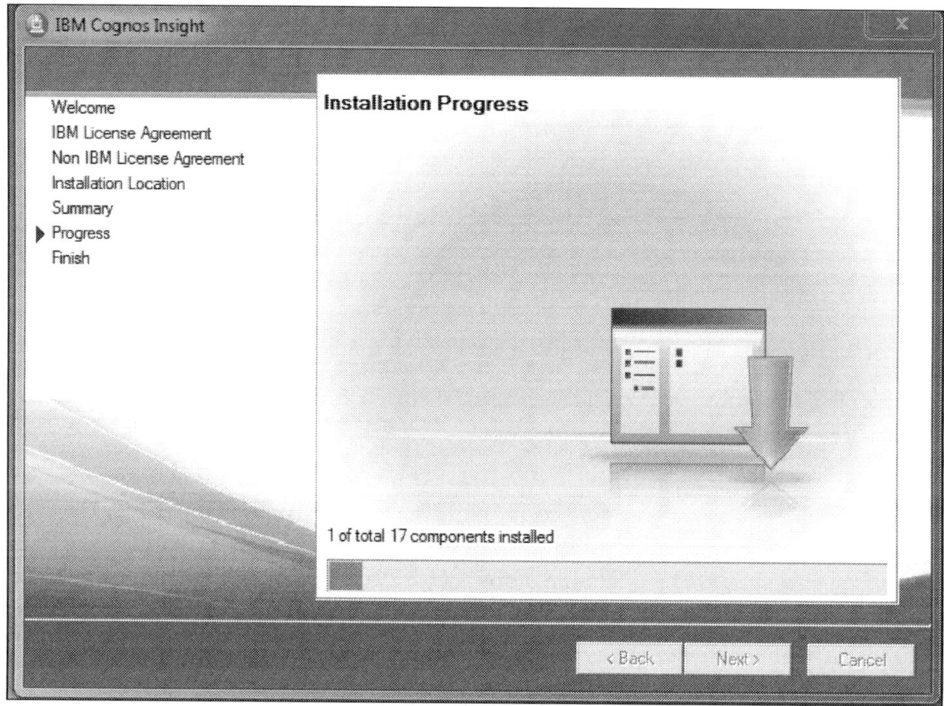

The following screenshot shows that the installation process is finished:

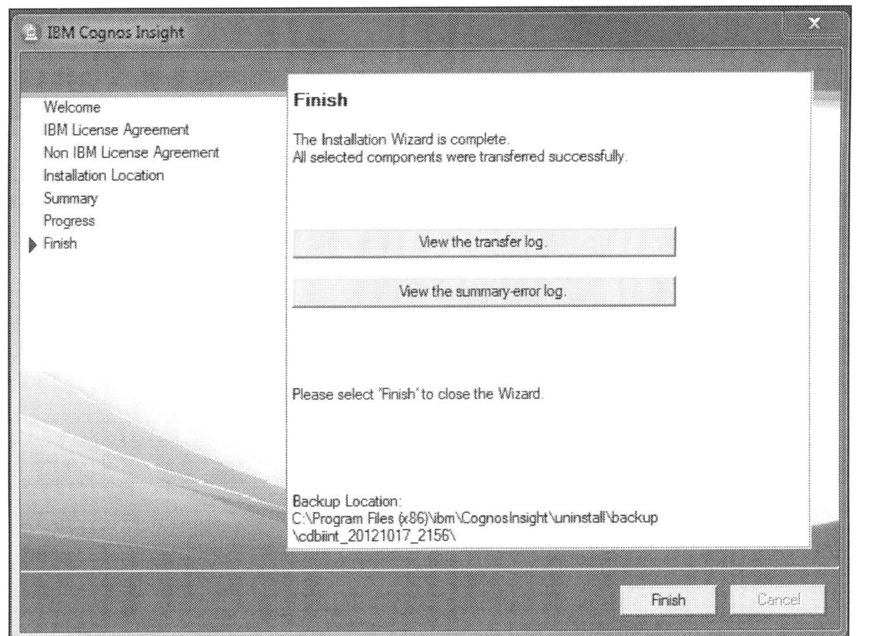

8. You can view the log files by clicking on the **View the transfer log** or **View the summary-error log** buttons to see each of the log files, as shown in the following screenshot:

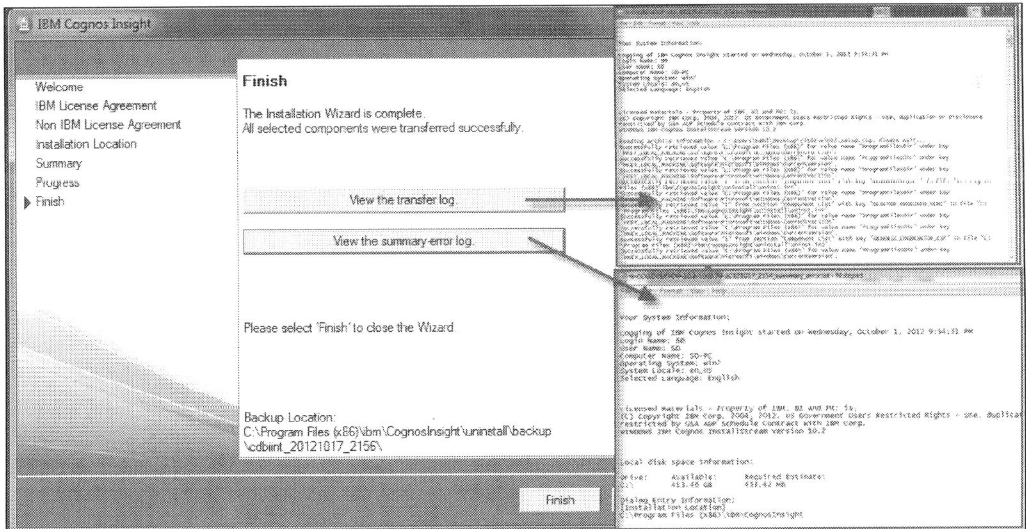

9. Once you click on **Finish**, the installation is completed and a shortcut to Cognos Insight is installed on the desktop. You can either access Cognos Insight Standard Edition by clicking on the shortcut icon on the desktop or navigate to **Start | Program Files | IBM Cognos Insight** to start the program.

The following screenshot shows the icon shortcut to IBM Cognos Insight created on the user's desktop machine:

To confirm that an install was successfully done, check that the following folders and files appear in the location as shown:

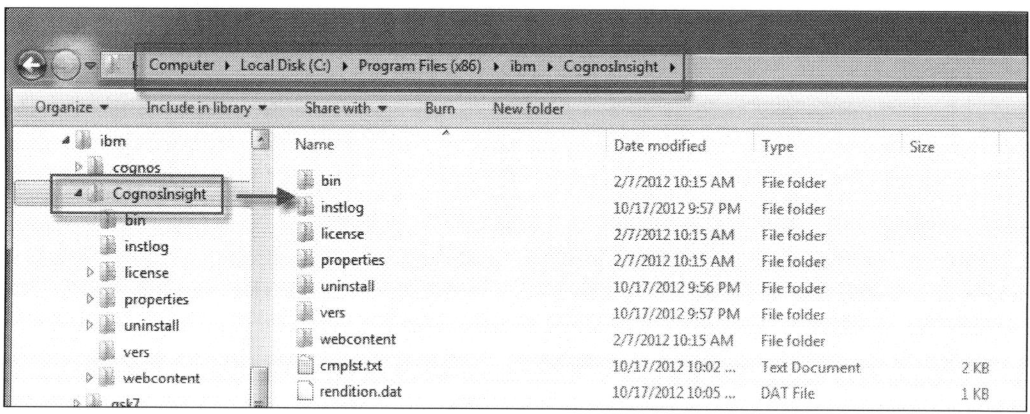

Installation of IBM Cognos Insight on an existing Cognos BI Environment

The prerequisites for a Provisioned install of Cognos Insight in an existing Cognos BI environment are as follows:

- Make sure that the version of Cognos BI is 10.1.1 or higher
- Cognos BI administrator should assign the targeted users the Enhanced Consumer role
- Disable browser pop-up blockers

For single server installs, where the gateway, Cognos application server, and the content, store are all the installs on the same server:

1. Stop all the Cognos services.
2. Install Cognos Insight successfully using the installation wizard.
3. Restart the Cognos services.
4. Cognos BI admin should assign the Enhanced Consumer role to the targeted users.
5. Cognos Insight will now be available in Cognos connection for those selected users.

For a distributed server install, the following are the steps to install Cognos Insight in a distributed environment. Follow these steps when installing Cognos Insight in a distributed environment:

1. Stop all the Cognos services.
2. Start the Cognos installation wizard.
3. Select the Cognos Insight BI Integration.
4. For all the Gateway machines, select Cognos Insight BI Integration Gateway.
5. Proceed with a successful install.
6. For all Cognos Application server machines, select Cognos Insight BI Integration.
7. Proceed with a successful install.
8. Restart the Cognos services.
9. Cognos BI Admin should assign Enhanced Consumer role to targeted users.
10. Cognos Insight will now be available in Cognos Connection for those users.

For remote installations, Cognos Insight can also be installed to multiple remote desktops using third-party network tools and command line codes that send the `CognosInsight.msi` file to target locations. This topic is out of bounds for this chapter.

Uninstalling IBM Cognos Insight

Here are the steps to uninstall Cognos Insight.

1. Cognos Insight Standard Edition can be uninstalled from the **Start Menu | Program Files | IBM Cognos Insight**, as shown in the following screenshot:

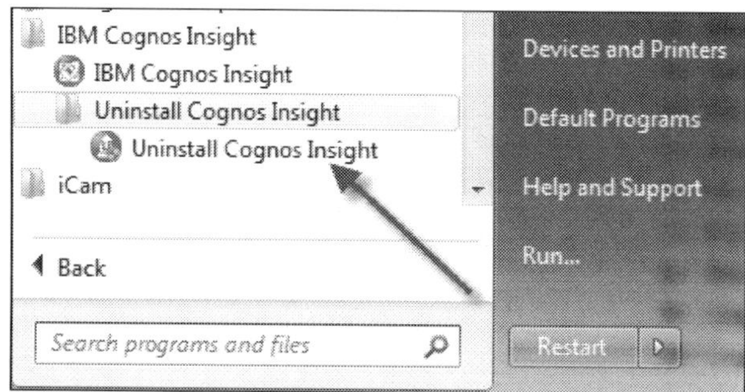

2. Follow the steps in the wizard and select the objects and components that need to be uninstalled. The **Uninstall Wizard** is shown in the following screenshot:

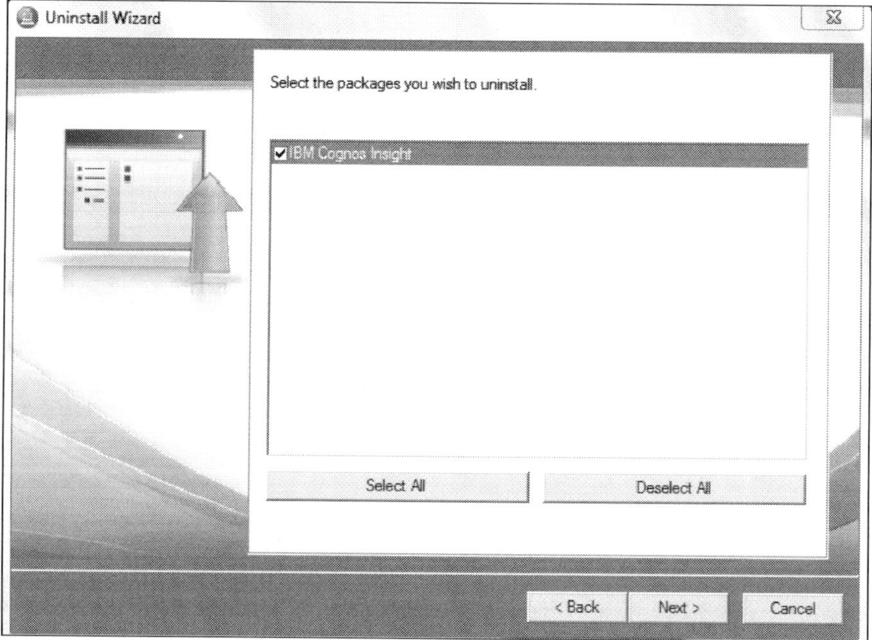

3. Uninstalling Cognos Insight for a provisioned install can be accomplished from the **Control Panel** in a Windows operating system. The following screenshot displays the **Control Panel** program in a Windows based operating system:

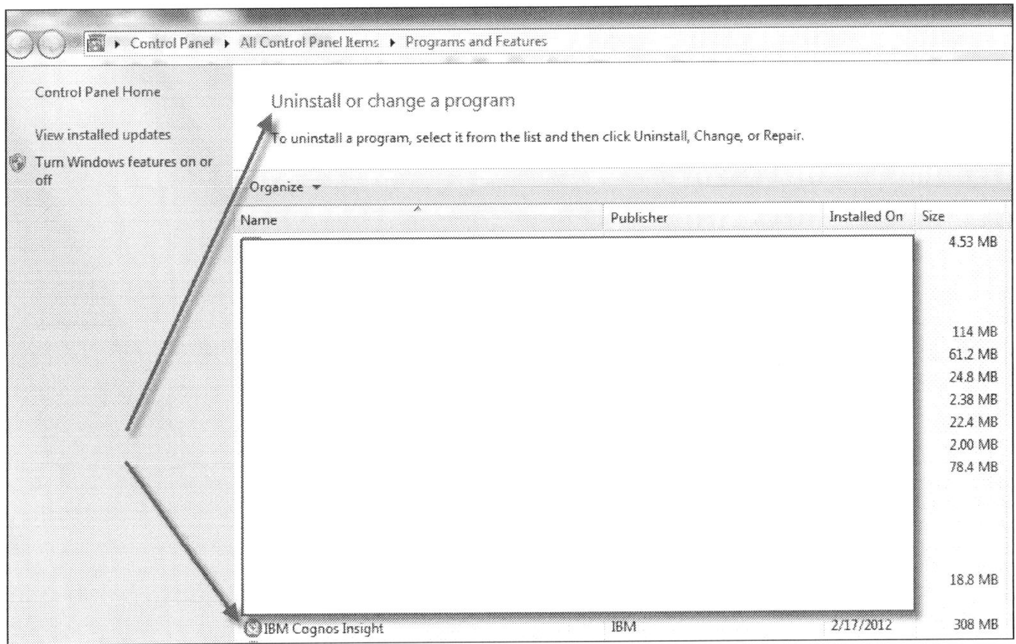

Connecting IBM Cognos Insight to the Cognos BI and IBM TM1 Environments

Connecting IBM Cognos Insight to Cognos BI and IBM TM1 is done by configuring the Cognos BI and TM1 link into Cognos Insight.

As shown in the following screenshot, from the **Actions** drop-down menu on the top left-hand side, select **Publish** and follow the wizard instructions:

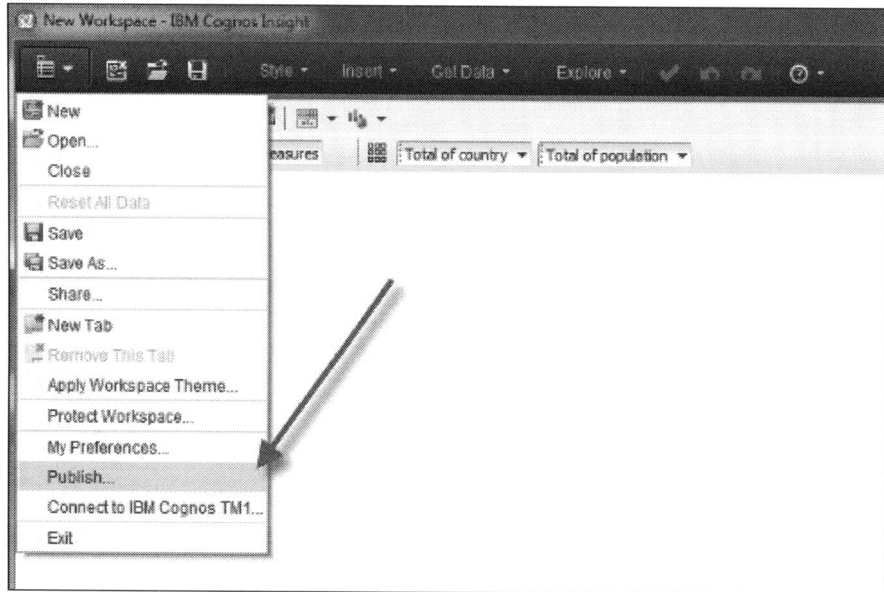

Input the connection string parameters, as shown in the next screenshot, into the **TM1 systems URL box** and click on **Finish**. Cognos Insight workspaces are then sent to the TM1 server and the users can access the Cognos Insight workspaces via Cognos Business Intelligence and Cognos Express.

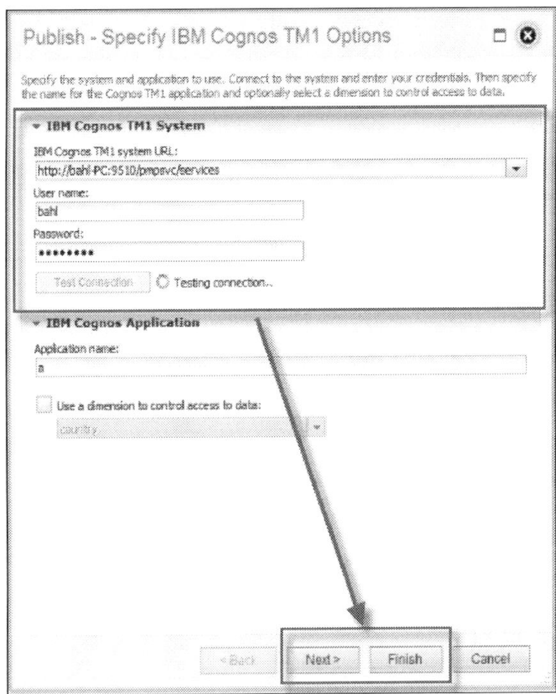

Sharing Cognos Insight workspaces into the Cognos BI environment requires the user to select **Share**. On the top left-hand side corner in Cognos Insight, click on the drop-down **Actions** menu and select **Share** (as shown in the following screenshot):

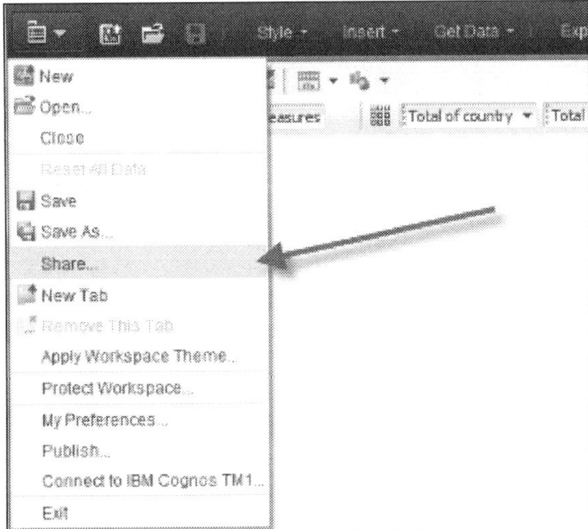

Follow the wizard; input the existing Cognos BI gateway as the required parameters. Depending on the security setup, a login/password might be required, as shown in the following screenshot:

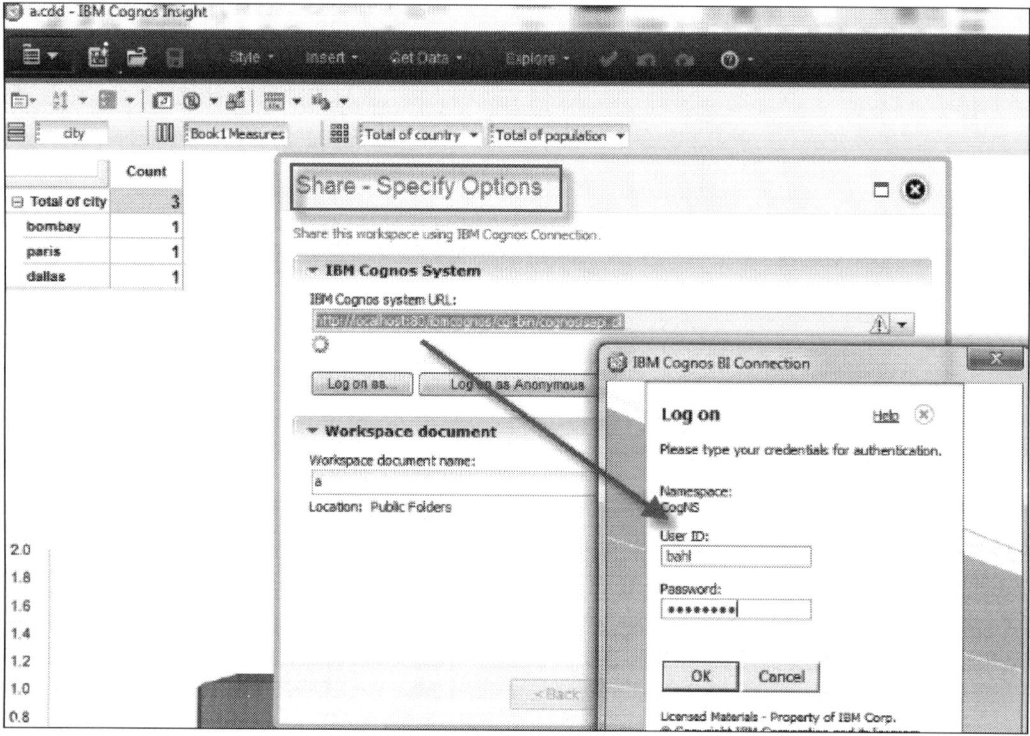

Once the credentials have been accepted, click on **Finish**. This will publish the Cognos Insight content into the Cognos Business Intelligence web portal, Cognos Connection. This deploys the workspace into Cognos connection and can now be shared with a broader group of users.

Configuring the Cognos BI and IBM TM1 URLs as part of the installation procedure under **Preferences** within Cognos Insight saves the URL information. This can be a time saver for the users, as the URLs are now available any time a "publish" is required.

Summary

Much like any other application install, a plan of action is necessary for a successful install. Following the steps described in this chapter will ensure a successful installation.

The next chapter will describe features such as importing, exploring, and analyzing the data sets within IBM Cognos Insight.

3
Usability of IBM Cognos Insight

Now that IBM Cognos Insight has been successfully installed as a desktop application, it is time to understand how to best use its features to import data, analyze it, and build workspaces. This chapter will describe how to bring in different data sources into Cognos Insight and use its functionalities to reorient, restructure, and display data in rich visual formats. In addition, the chapter will demonstrate the sandbox functionality for write-back scenario based planning and analysis.

Before we begin, it is important to understand the basic concepts of OLAP Technology. Online Analytical Processing (OLAP) is a data structure in the form of a cube. The simplest cube can be created using two dimensions and one measure. Dimensions are a stack of similar data grouped together such as region, product, or time. A dimension is comprised of various levels that structure the dimension in a form of a hierarchy. Take an example of the regions dimension, which may have levels such as country, state, district, and city; or the example of a time dimension that might have levels such as year, quarter, month, week, and day. This hierarchical structure enables users to drill down and drill up on the cube, thereby giving summary and detail levels within the same structure. Furthermore, a member is defined as the data within the level. Members within the country level of a region's dimension would include USA, France, England, Japan, and so on. Members of a time dimension across all levels would be 2012, Quarter 4, November, Week 47, 23rd day of the month.

Dimensions add context to the measures and without context, measures are meaningless numbers. They are quantitative data items that give a numeric value to the data, such as revenue, cost of goods sold, profit margin, net sales, discounts, employee headcount, and so on, that eventually drive the performance metrics and set goals.

By contrast, an attribute in OLAP is an additional piece of information about data in a cube that provides descriptive information. Product color or product size would be attributes for the product dimension, month name would be an attribute of the month level in a time dimension, and so on. OLAP cubes are the foundations of IBM Cognos Insight and are used to answer the 4 Ws: *what, who, when,* and *where,* using the combination of dimensions and measures. Relate these questions to any data set and they provide the key analysis that Cognos Insight can derive for your organization.

A multi-dimensional analysis would then be considered as one with more than two dimensions and measures in a cube structure that enables analysis of the data from various perspectives. This technology makes a true multi-dimensional analysis.

Importing data into IBM Cognos Insight

To begin with any analysis, importing data into IBM Cognos Insight is the first step. The following are three possible methods to accomplish this:

- **Drag and drop (Quick Import method)**: This method allows spreadsheets (Excel files), CSV files, or existing Cognos Insight Workspaces (cdd file extensions) to be dropped onto the Cognos Insight interface. The smart-metadata capability automatically creates a highly compressed OLAP cube structure with dimensions, levels, measures, and the relationships between them based on the data in the file. As per the following screenshot, a spreadsheet containing the US Economic Census for the Mining Industry is dropped onto the application. JPG images can also be dropped in the similar manner to show the image on Cognos Insight.

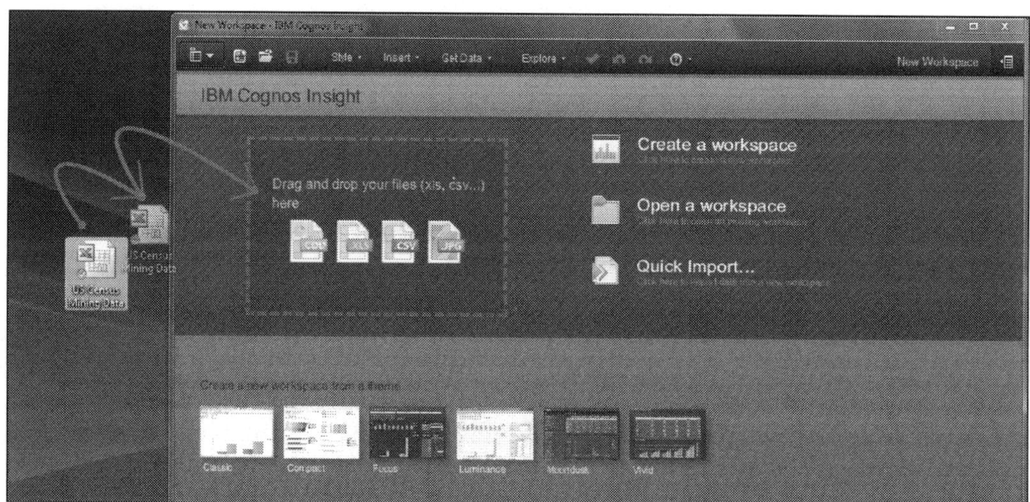

Alternatively, the *Quick Import method* brings up a window from where file selections can be made. This option can be accessed by selecting **Get Data | Quick Import...** or by selecting **Quick Import** from the startup screen, as shown in the following screenshot:

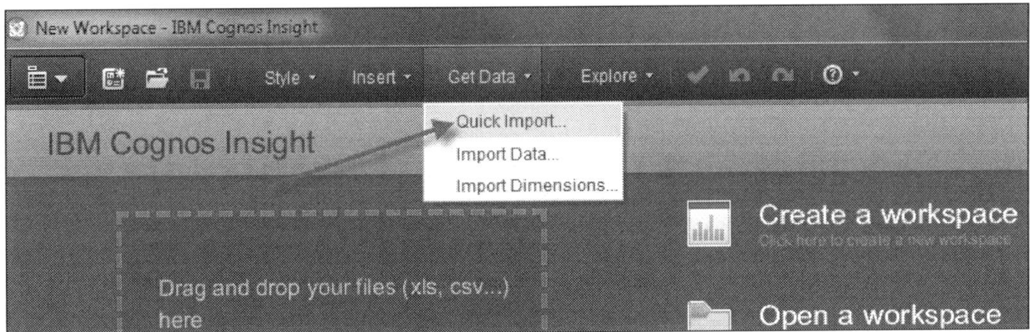

The following is a screenshot of the data in the file:

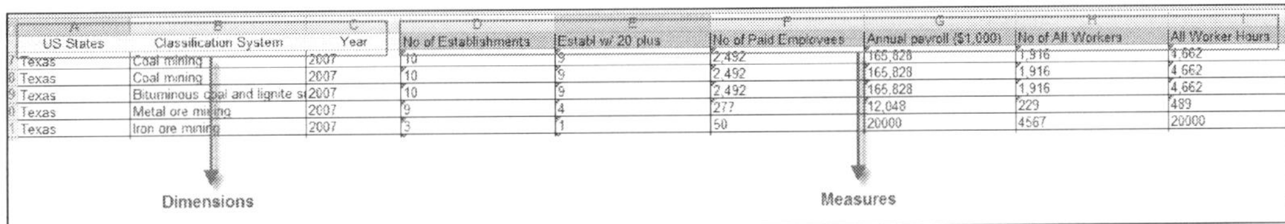

US States	Classification System	Year	No of Establishments	Establ w/ 20 plus	No of Paid Employees	Annual payroll ($1,000)	No of All Workers	All Worker Hours
Texas	Coal mining	2007	10	9	2,492	165,828	1,916	4,662
Texas	Coal mining	2007	10	9	2,492	165,828	1,916	4,662
Texas	Bituminous coal and lignite s	2007	10	9	2,492	165,828	1,916	4,662
Texas	Metal ore mining	2007	9	4	277	12,048	229	489
Texas	Iron ore mining	2007	3	1	50	20000	4567	20000

A quick look at the source file shows IBM Cognos Insight recognizing the first three columns and their data to be type text and defines them as **Dimensions** in the cube. The smart-metadata enables the import wizard to differentiate data types within the columns as measureable or non-measureable values such as Number of Paid Employees versus customer number. The remaining columns in the data source are numeric in nature; these comprise of the **Measures** within the OLAP cube. For purely analysis purposes, the data is now represented in Cognos Insight in the form of a crosstab or pivot table with rows and columns.

The following screenshot shows a crosstab and a chart of the data imported into Cognos Insight. This representation is displayed in a **widget** or container that resides on the workspace. The various dimensions and measures are displayed on the title bar which allow the slicing and dicing of data for analysis purposes. Slicing and dicing in OLAP terminology refers to focusing on a particular data set by changing the original orientation and then filtering certain aspects of the new desired orientation.

The widget has some additional properties that will be discussed later in the chapter. This and other widgets lie on a tab sheet. A workspace in Cognos Insight can have multiple tabs.

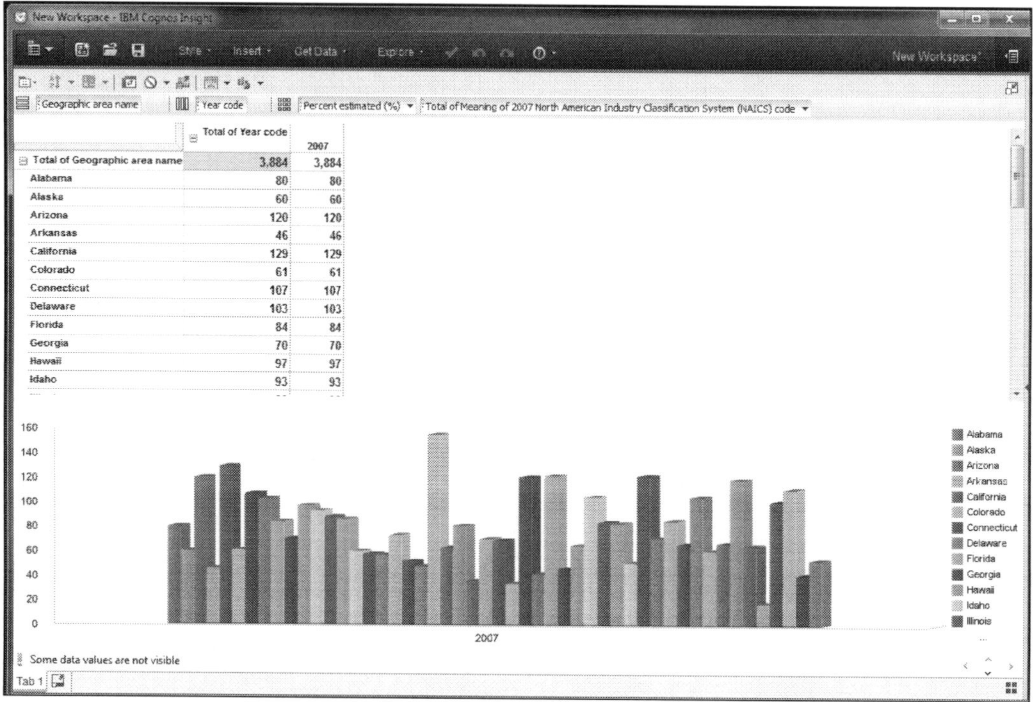

- **Import Wizard method**: When importing various types of data structures and sources, Cognos Insight has a built-in import wizard. This wizard can be accessed by the **Get Data** tool bar menu and selecting **Import Data...** or **Import Dimensions...**, as shown in the following screenshot:

The difference between selecting either the **Import Data...** or **Import Dimensions...** option depends on the source data. Use the former when data has dimensions and measures, while the latter is used when importing only dimensions.

There are four types of **Data Source** that exist to allow for importing multiple data sources:

- File
- Relational Data Source (ODBC)
- IBM Cognos Report Data
- IBM Cognos Package Data

The highlighted section in the following screenshot shows the import wizard's multiple data type options:

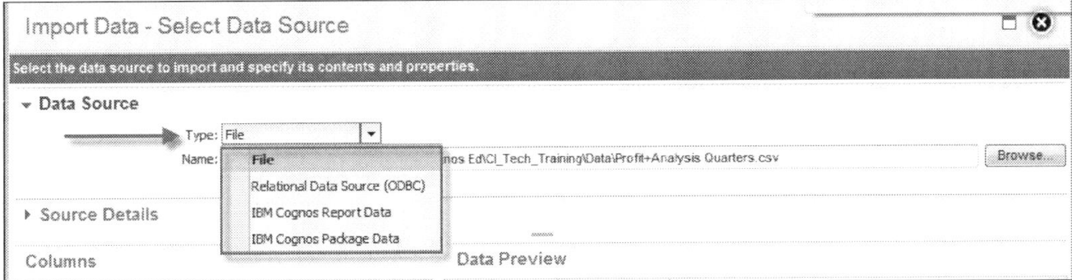

The following screenshot shows the **Source Details** options when importing data. As shown under the **Source Details** section, importing data across various options exist to accommodate the data format. These options can also be used to select or deselect columns within the data source, thereby giving the import process the flexibility to bring in relevant data only.

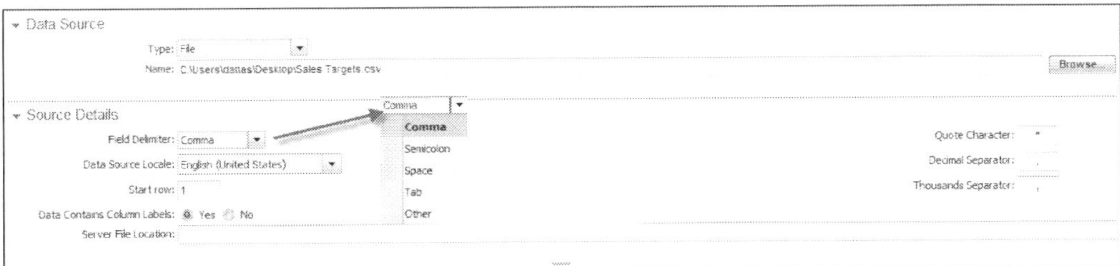

When importing a file, the smart-metadata within the import wizard can identify the data type and automatically roll up logical levels for measures. An example of this would be when the smart-metadata algorithm creates links to the data and displays the data as natural hierarchies of product line to product type to product or year to quarter to month. As shown in the following screenshot, the data type is of a crosstab or pivot table. The import wizard then provides the following options to bring in the appropriate data structure with the flexibility to select the data range within the source file:

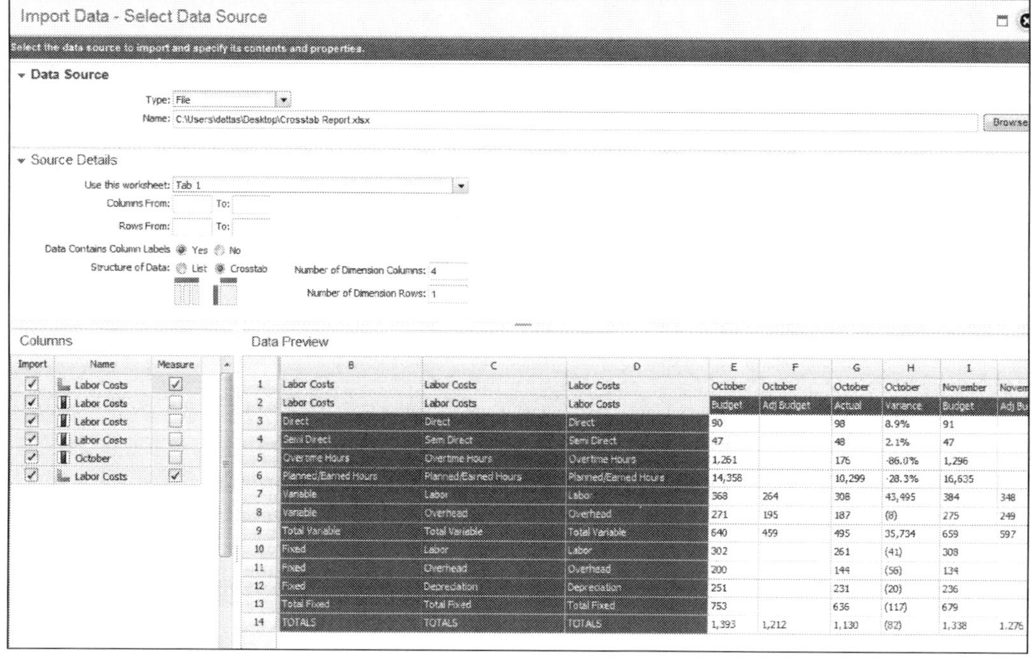

	B	C	D	E	F	G	H	I	
1	Labor Costs	Labor Costs	Labor Costs	October	October	October	October	November	Novem
2	Labor Costs	Labor Costs	Labor Costs	Budget	Adj Budget	Actual	Variance	Budget	Adj Bu
3	Direct	Direct	Direct	90		98	8.9%	91	
4	Semi Direct	Semi Direct	Semi Direct	47		48	2.1%	47	
5	Overtime Hours	Overtime Hours	Overtime Hours	1,261		176	-86.0%	1,296	
6	Planned/Earned Hours	Planned/Earned Hours	Planned/Earned Hours	14,358		10,299	-28.3%	16,635	
7	Variable	Labor	Labor	368	264	308	43,495	384	348
8	Variable	Overhead	Overhead	271	195	187	(8)	275	249
9	Total Variable	Total Variable	Total Variable	640	459	495	35,734	659	597
10	Fixed	Labor	Labor	302		261	(41)	308	
11	Fixed	Overhead	Overhead	200		144	(56)	134	
12	Fixed	Depreciation	Depreciation	251		231	(20)	236	
13	Total Fixed	Total Fixed	Total Fixed	753		636	(117)	679	
14	TOTALS	TOTALS	TOTALS	1,393	1,212	1,130	(82)	1,338	1,276

Users also have the ability to connect to an ODBC connection. Cognos Insight can import data from multiple vendor applications, such as Microsoft Access, SQL Server, dBASE files, and so on. If looking to leverage predictive data or other kinds of relational data sources, one can connect through this method as shown in the following screenshot:

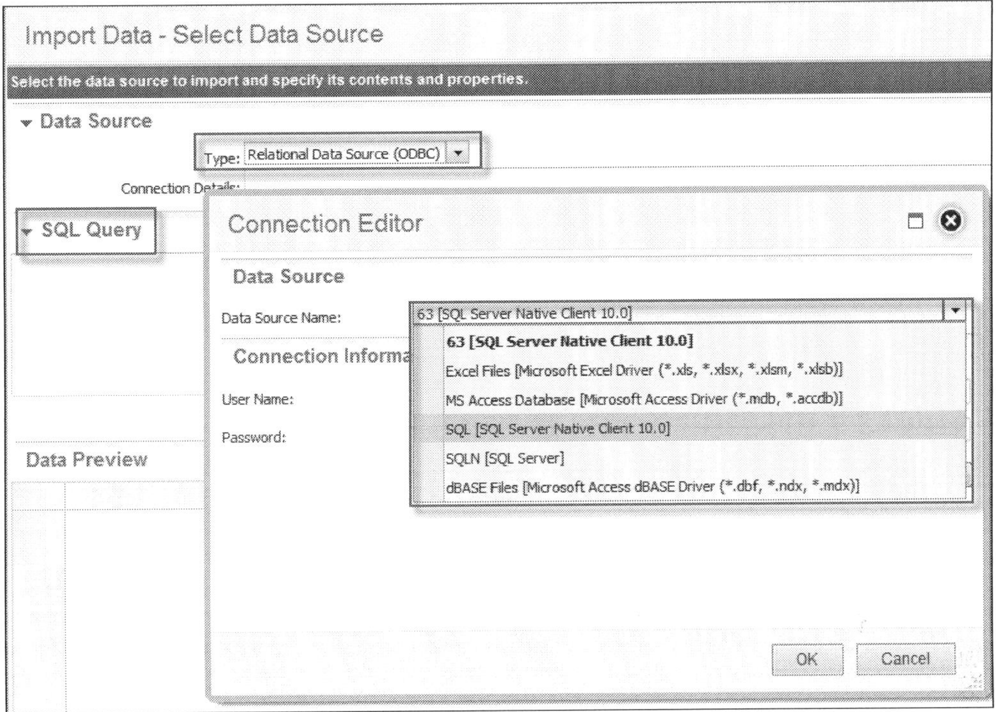

Under the **SQL Query** window, input SQL commands to access the data or use the **Query Builder** to drag and drop tables from the **Metadata Explorer**, create the relationships between the tables, and specify the cardinalities as shown in the following screenshot:

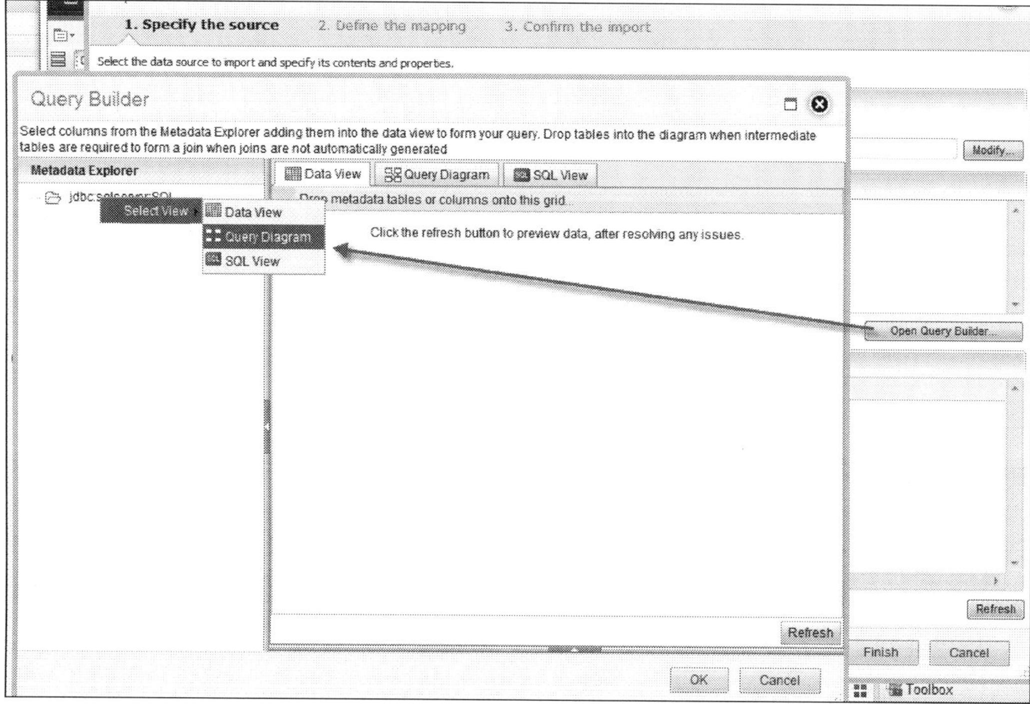

IBM Cognos Insight also connects to an organization's existing Cognos Business Intelligence (BI) environment to leverage trusted BI data via list reports. Once the correct parameters (Gateway URI link and valid credentials) have been entered, a new window allows browsing for specific reports and selecting them as a data source. If the reports have prompts, ensure the prompt selections have been satisfied and the report is in a tabular format.

A **Data Preview** window will show the report data to be imported, as shown in the following screenshot:

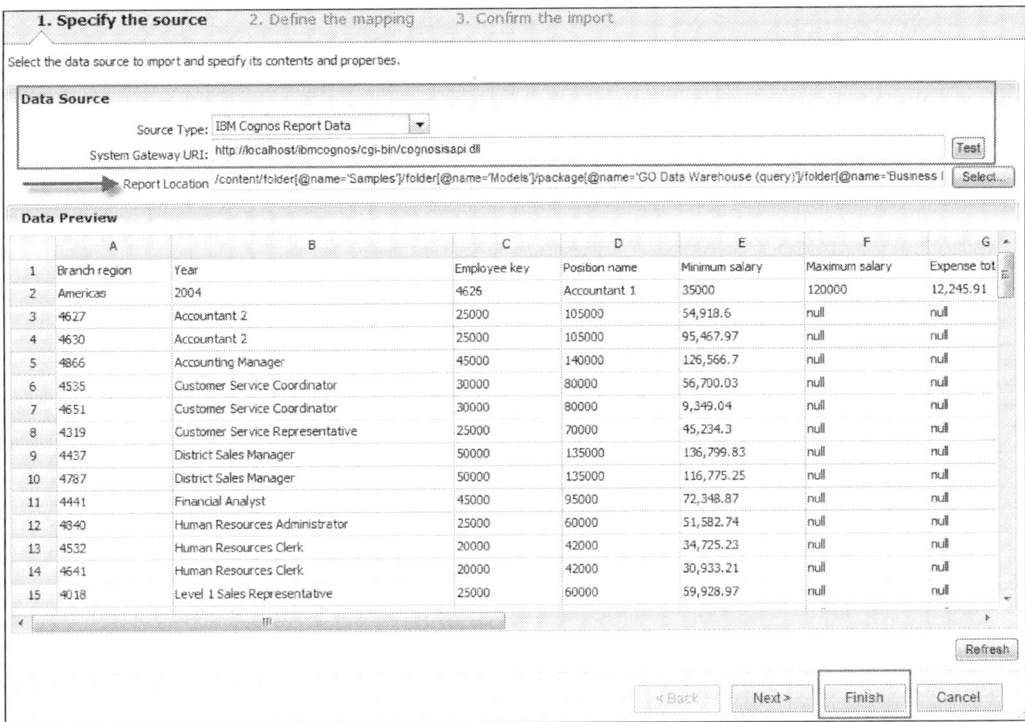

Data Source

Source Type:	IBM Cognos Report Data
System Gateway URI:	http://localhost/ibmcognos/cgi-bin/cognosisapi.dll
Report Location	/content/folder[@name='Samples']/folder[@name='Models']/package[@name='GO Data Warehouse (query)']/folder[@name='Business ...

Data Preview

	A	B	C	D	E	F	G
1	Branch region	Year	Employee key	Position name	Minimum salary	Maximum salary	Expense tot
2	Americas	2004	4626	Accountant 1	35000	120000	12,245.91
3	4627	Accountant 2	25000	105000	54,918.6	null	null
4	4630	Accountant 2	25000	105000	95,467.97	null	null
5	4866	Accounting Manager	45000	140000	126,566.7	null	null
6	4535	Customer Service Coordinator	30000	80000	56,700.03	null	null
7	4651	Customer Service Coordinator	30000	80000	9,349.04	null	null
8	4319	Customer Service Representative	25000	70000	45,234.3	null	null
9	4437	District Sales Manager	50000	135000	136,799.83	null	null
10	4787	District Sales Manager	50000	135000	116,775.25	null	null
11	4441	Financial Analyst	45000	95000	72,348.87	null	null
12	4840	Human Resources Administrator	25000	60000	51,582.74	null	null
13	4532	Human Resources Clerk	20000	42000	34,725.23	null	null
14	4641	Human Resources Clerk	20000	42000	30,933.21	null	null
15	4018	Level 1 Sales Representative	25000	60000	59,928.97	null	null

Refresh

« Back   Next >   Finish   Cancel

Lastly, Cognos Insight connects to the existing IBM Cognos packages. In order to connect to the BI environment, select the package location and name. Then choose the query subjects that will provide data for the analysis and preview the selection in the window pane.

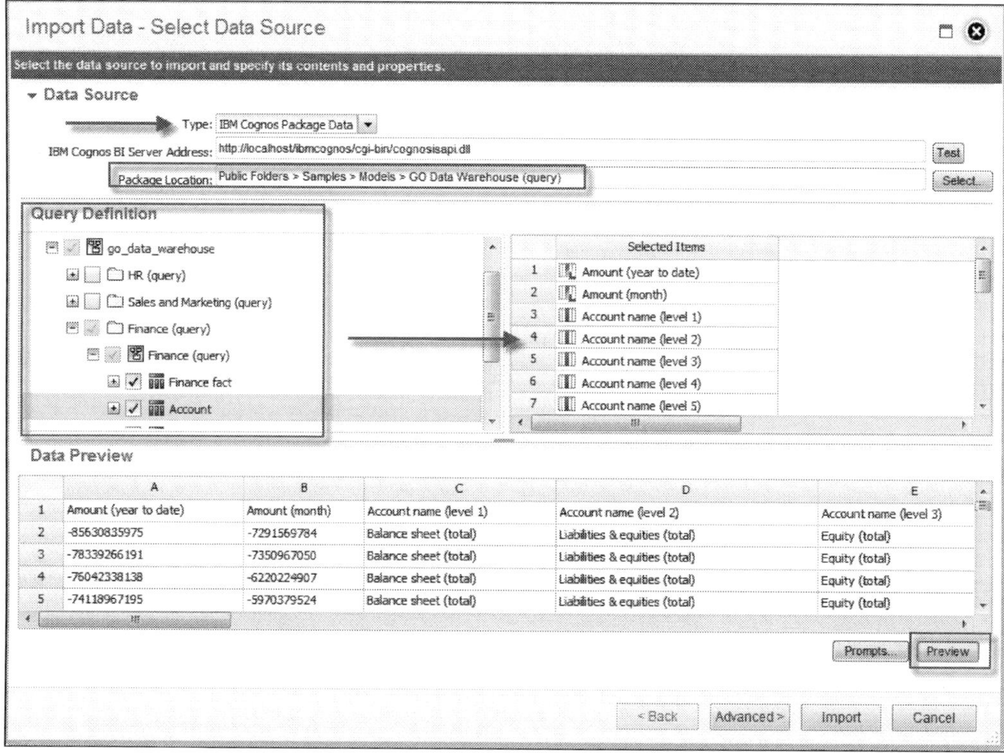

The **Advanced>** icon at the bottom of the wizard provides options to map the importing data. The mapping portion of the import wizard provides a **Data Preview** at the top and the mapping information at the bottom half of the window. Use the bottom half section to build dimensions and levels by dragging the source columns (on the left-hand side) into the target columns (on the right-hand side).

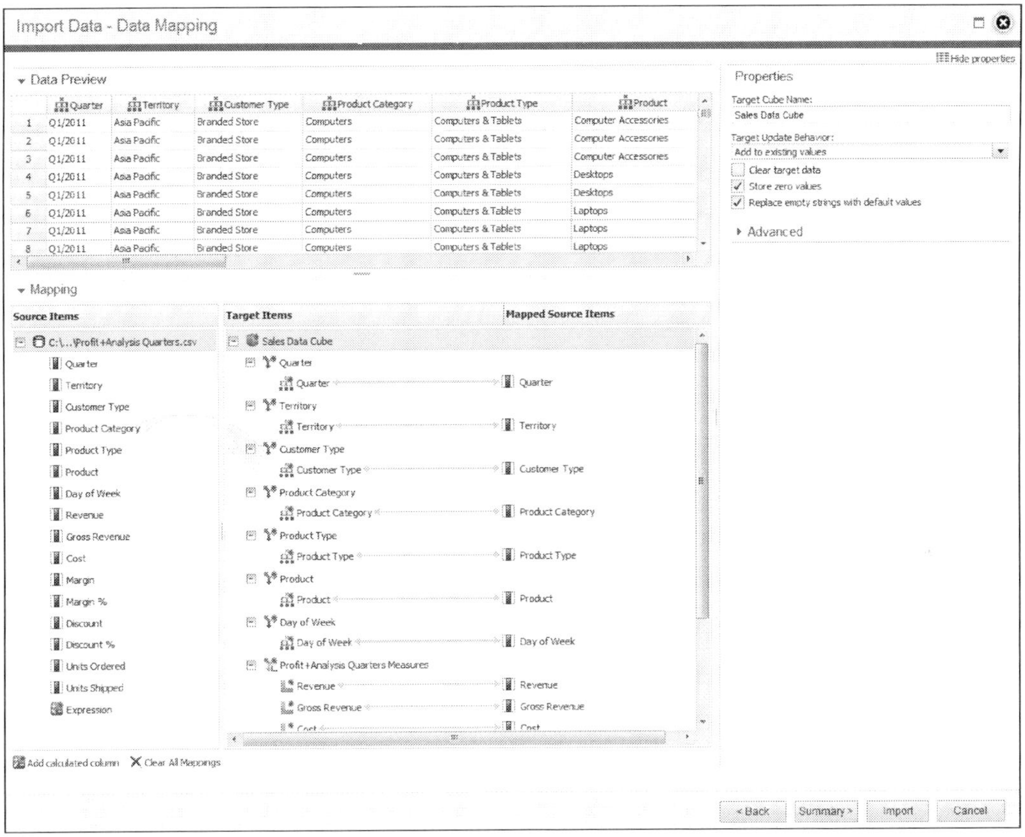

Each of the columns under the **Source Items** (right-click) can be used in the analysis as dimensions, measures, levels, and attributes.

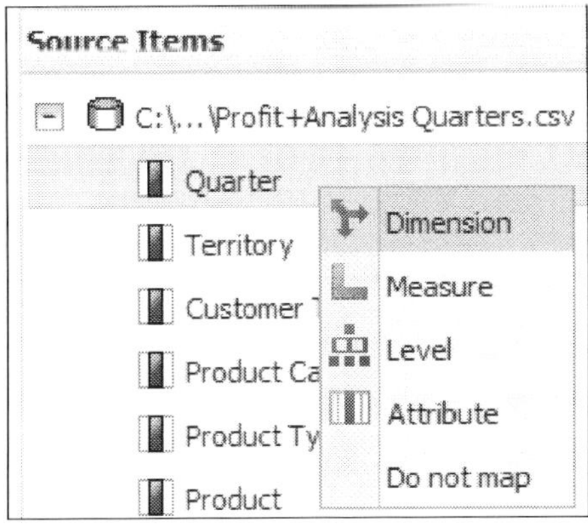

Use the **Properties** window on the right-hand side to add the **Target Cube Name** and specify the data import behavior type. From the following screenshot, selecting **Add to existing values** adds the newly imported data to the target cube, while the other option replaces the older values with the newly imported values:

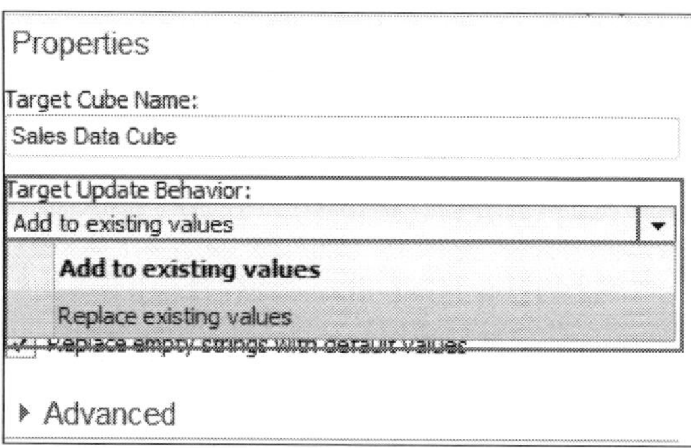

As shown in the following screenshot, other options such as **Clear target data**, **Store zero values**, and **Replace empty strings with default values**, assist in refining the import process.

The **Advanced** option, as shown in the following screenshot, allows the usage of existing OLAP cube components (dimensions and measures) to be included in the importing of new data:

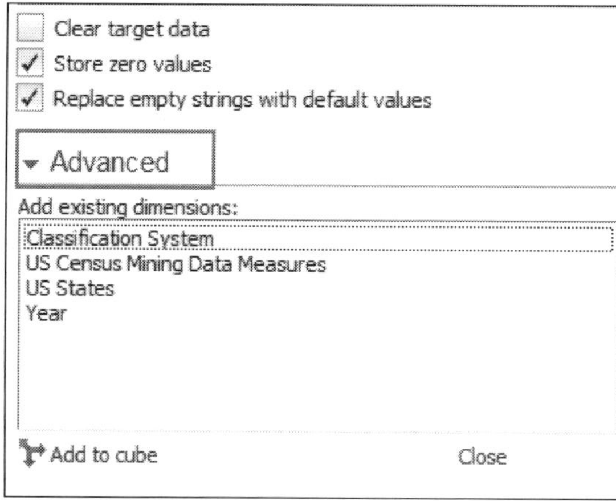

Next select **Summary** to see a list of import messages and the property summary of each object being imported into Cognos Insight. Finally, the **Import** button will close the wizard and import data based on the user's selection.

- **Data Refresh method**: There are two methods of refreshing existing data in Cognos Insight: **Silent Refresh** and **Guided Refresh**. These options are cube specific and can be accessed from the content icon on the top right of the application as shown in the following screenshot:

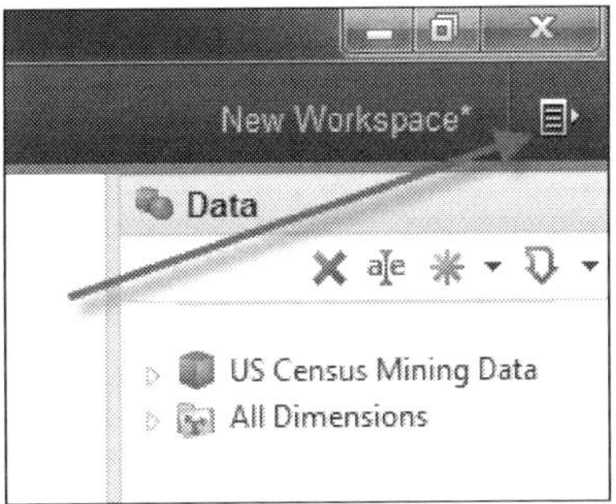

This provides the set of options for a guided or silent refresh as shown in the following screenshot:

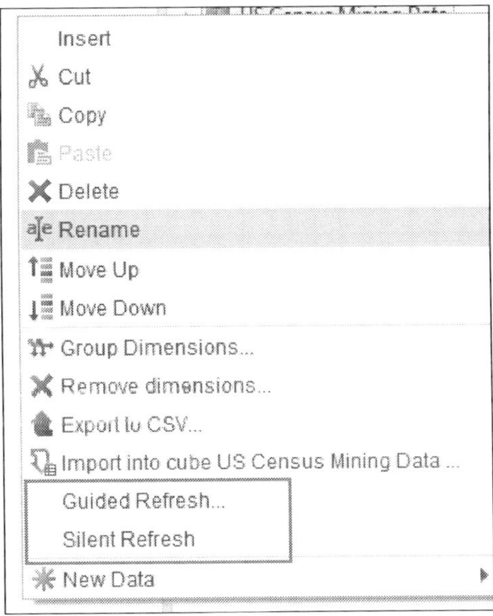

Select **Silent Refresh** when the data has been modified in the data source and Cognos Insight is aware of the location of the data source. This option is selected when there is no change to the metadata, meaning no columns have been added or deleted from the source. While the mappings are unchanged, this option will refresh the data in Cognos Insight.

Use **Guided Refresh** when the source data has been modified in terms of the data structure. This will bring up the import wizard that will provide the flexibility in importing data. Follow the wizard, as described earlier, to bring in the new data structure as required.

Reorienting data into Cognos Insight

Cognos Insight provides rich visualization options to raw data and allows us to drill up and down on crosstabs or various available charts. The crosstabs and charts provide interactivity with the data to allow further analysis that leads to deeper insights.

This section will describe the various features used to reorient the data in a fashion that suits the user's needs.

- Drag-and-drop dimensions
- Slice and dice title dimensions
- Nesting dimensions
- Sorting on data
- Swap rows and columns
- Charting options
- Filtering values/explorer points
- Types of calculations
- Writing rules
- Formatting methods
- Grouping dimensions

US Economic Census and IBM Cognos data have been used to build these examples.

Drag-and-drop dimensions

Changing the orientation of the cube can reveal many more answers in a multi-dimensional analysis. In Cognos Insight, drag-and-drop the title dimensions over either a row dimension or column dimension to change the existing view of the cube into a new view.

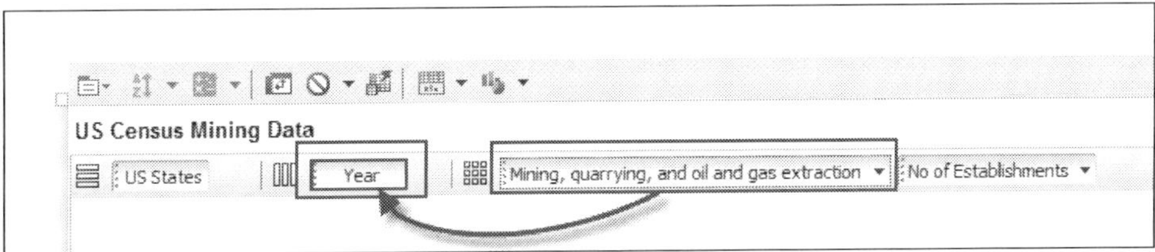

As shown in the previous screenshot, the **Year** dimension will be replaced with the **classification** dimension by dragging and dropping the **classification** dimension over the **Year** dimension.

Slice and dice title dimensions

Typical to OLAP applications, the slice and dice functionality will, in a way, present a specific cube view with a desired positioning order of the dimensions and filter this dimensional data specific to an OLAP member. The dimensional member values of a cube are referred to as the OLAP "edge" while the body of a cube contains the measure values. In this case, from the measures dimension, slice to the measure **Annual payroll ($1,000)**. This will change the data focus from **No of Establishments** to payroll information, without changing the row and column dimensions.

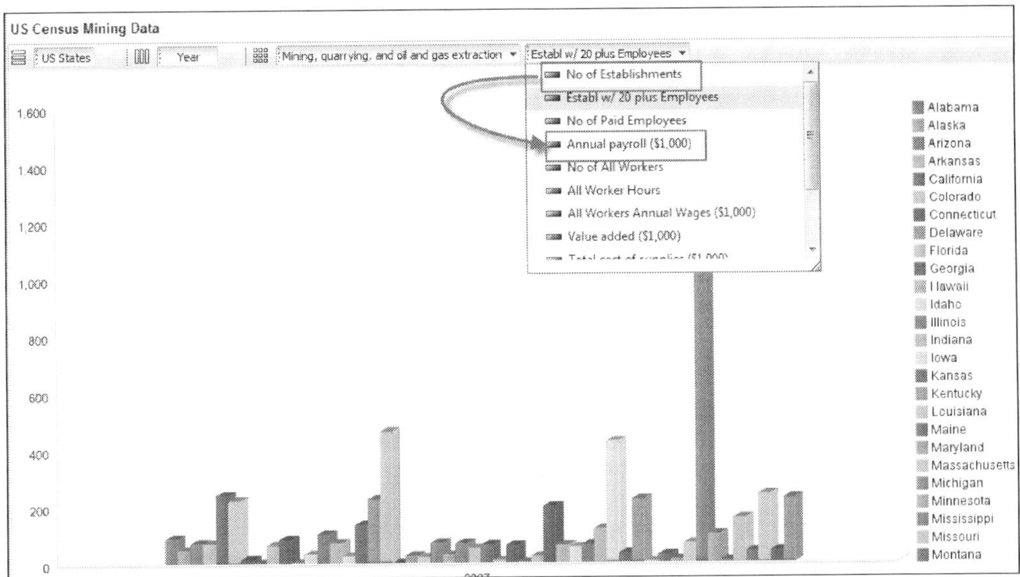

Nesting dimensions

Nesting dimensions or stacking them side by side, provides additional information to the cube view. Nesting dimensions allows two or more dimensions stacked in a row and/or column dimension to show data from multiple perspectives within the same cube view, thereby maximizing the real estate available on the page with data values.

In the following screenshot, **Total of Customer Type** title dimension is moved over and stacked to the right-hand side of the **Territory** row dimension:

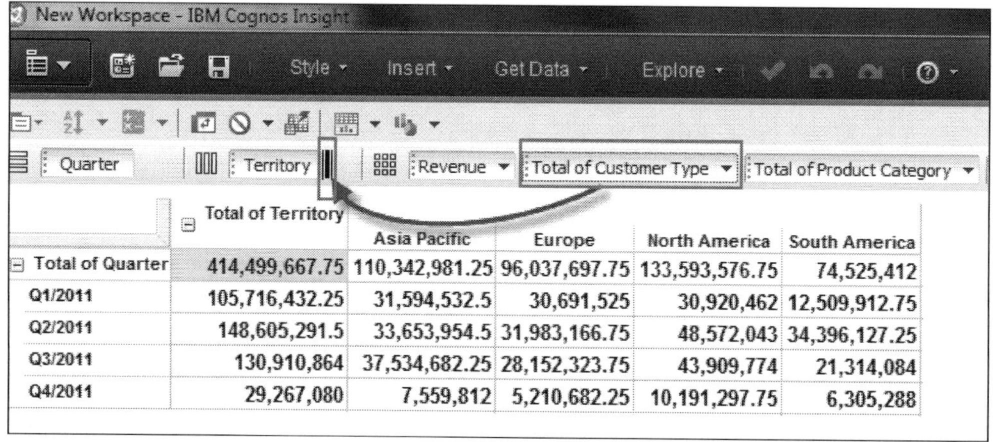

	Total of Territory	Asia Pacific	Europe	North America	South America
Total of Quarter	414,499,667.75	110,342,981.25	96,037,697.75	133,593,576.75	74,525,412
Q1/2011	105,716,432.25	31,594,532.5	30,691,525	30,920,462	12,509,912.75
Q2/2011	148,605,291.5	33,653,954.5	31,983,166.75	48,572,043	34,396,127.25
Q3/2011	130,910,864	37,534,682.25	28,152,323.75	43,909,774	21,314,084
Q4/2011	29,267,080	7,559,812	5,210,682.25	10,191,297.75	6,305,288

The following screenshot shows the resulting output:

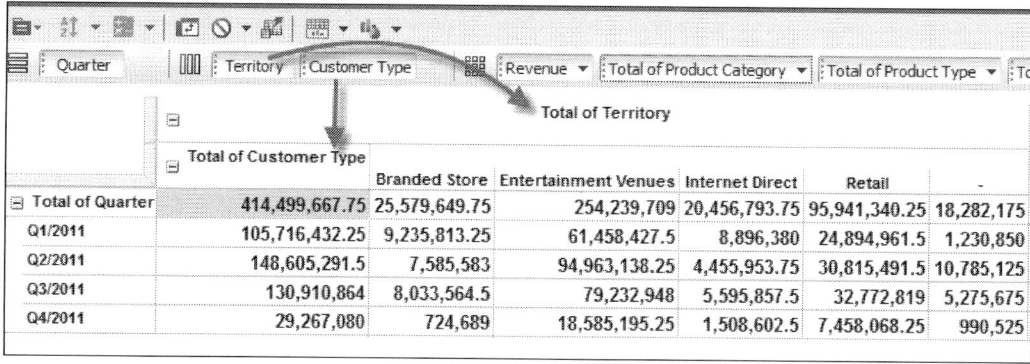

	Total of Customer Type	Branded Store	Entertainment Venues	Internet Direct	Retail	-
Total of Quarter	414,499,667.75	25,579,649.75	254,239,709	20,456,793.75	95,941,340.25	18,282,175
Q1/2011	105,716,432.25	9,235,813.25	61,458,427.5	8,896,380	24,894,961.5	1,230,850
Q2/2011	148,605,291.5	7,585,583	94,963,138.25	4,455,953.75	30,815,491.5	10,785,125
Q3/2011	130,910,864	8,033,564.5	79,232,948	5,595,857.5	32,772,819	5,275,675
Q4/2011	29,267,080	724,689	18,585,195.25	1,508,602.5	7,458,068.25	990,525

As can be noted, the **Quarter** dimension displays information in the rows (row dimension), while the column dimension is now nested with **Territory** type and **Customer Type** dimension. The **Territory** type dimension acts as the parent and displays only the customers available under specific territories.

Sorting of data

The sorting of dimensional data in Cognos Insight can be done on the row or column dimension. Select the row or column dimension on which sorting is to be applied and right click on the **header**.

In the following screenshot, **Sort by Label** (**Ascending** or **Descending**) will sort alphabetically on the names of the states. **Sort by Value** will sort based on the data values for the states.

Don't Sort cancels any sorting on the dimensional row or column.

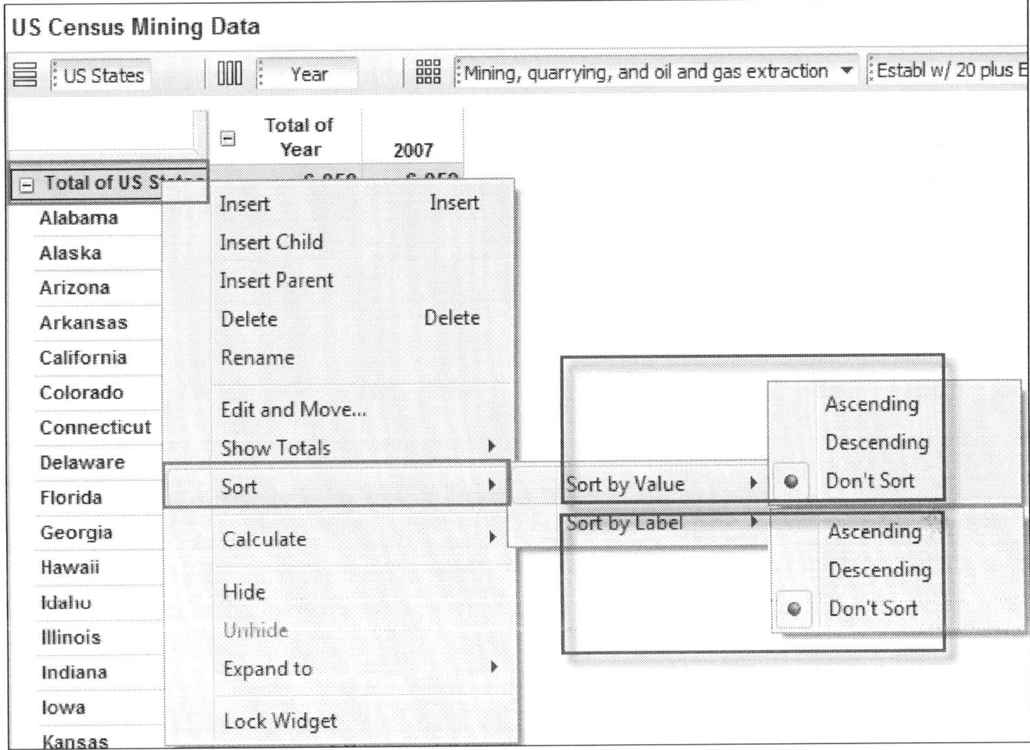

The following screenshot displays the **Sort by Label** result on the **US States** row dimension by descending order:

US States	Year	Mining, quarrying, and oil ar

	Total of Year	2007
Total of US States	**6,059**	6,059
Wyoming	227	227
Wisconsin	43	43
West Virginia	240	240
Washington	41	41
Virginia	157	157
Vermont	7	7
Utah	100	100
Texas	1,483	1,483
Tennessee	68	68
South Dakota	13	13
South Carolina	29	29
Rhode Island	6	6
Pennsylvania	224	224

Swap rows and columns

Swapping rows and columns is a feature that reorients the rows with the columns in the existing cube view. This is used to give an improved view for analysis when too many data elements exist in the current combination of row and column dimension. The following screenshot shows the **Territory** dimension and the **Quarter** by week column dimension. This is a busy view that makes visual at-a-glance analysis a challenge. Leveraging the swap row and column feature will change the view by swapping the rows with the columns.

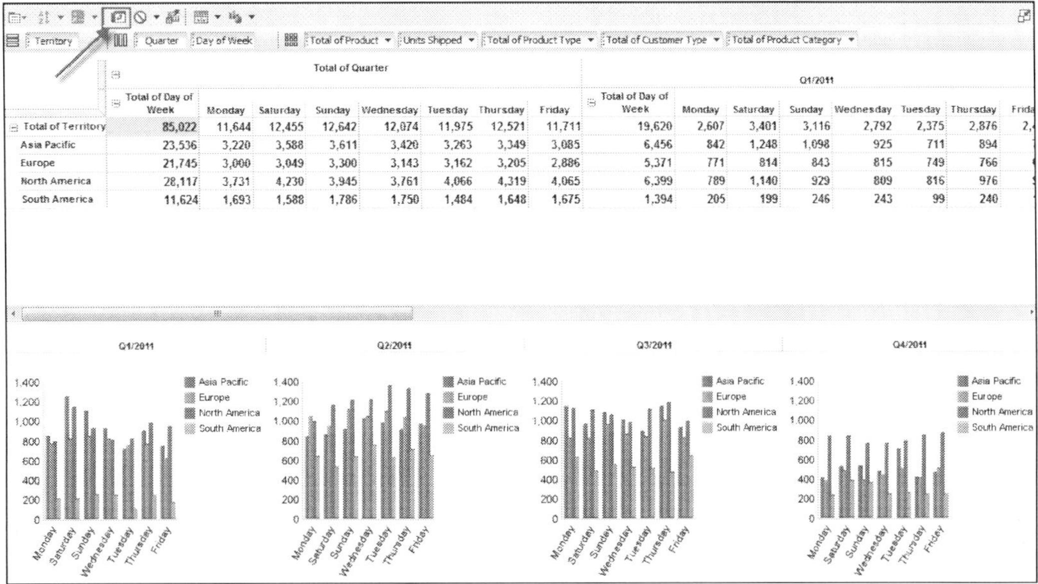

The following screenshot shows the swapped rows and columns. The stacked
columns have now moved to the row dimension level and the graph is easier to read.

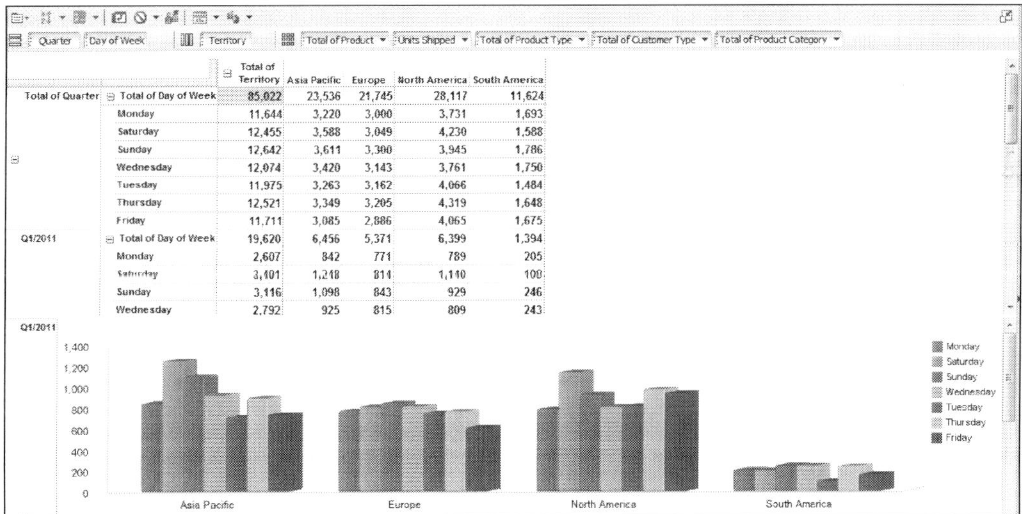

		Total of Territory	Asia Pacific	Europe	North America	South America
Total of Quarter	Total of Day of Week	85,022	23,536	21,745	28,117	11,624
	Monday	11,644	3,220	3,000	3,731	1,693
	Saturday	12,455	3,588	3,049	4,230	1,588
	Sunday	12,642	3,611	3,300	3,945	1,786
	Wednesday	12,074	3,420	3,143	3,761	1,750
	Tuesday	11,975	3,263	3,162	4,066	1,484
	Thursday	12,521	3,349	3,205	4,319	1,648
	Friday	11,711	3,085	2,886	4,065	1,675
Q1/2011	Total of Day of Week	19,620	6,456	5,371	6,399	1,394
	Monday	2,607	842	771	789	205
	Saturday	3,101	1,248	814	1,140	100
	Sunday	3,116	1,098	843	929	246
	Wednesday	2,792	925	815	809	243

Charting options

In Cognos Insight, there are numerous types of charts. Charts act as visual displays and in many cases, can display analysis better than textual data.

The previous screenshot can be simplified for the Analyst user by clicking on the **Change Chart** icon on the widget. The view of the chart now displays units shipped by day across all territories. Additionally, data can be directly added to charts from the content pane. Depending on the type of data in the analysis, Cognos Insight provides other chart types, such as **Area** charts, **Bar**, or **Column** charts, **Tree Map** that display hierarchies as nested rectangles, **Line** charts to display data as a series of points, and **Pie** or **Point** charts to display positive numerical values. Suitable colors can be selected from the **Palettes** option. To hide or show the legends, series, categories, grid lines, headers, and the like, select **View Options** for each chart type.

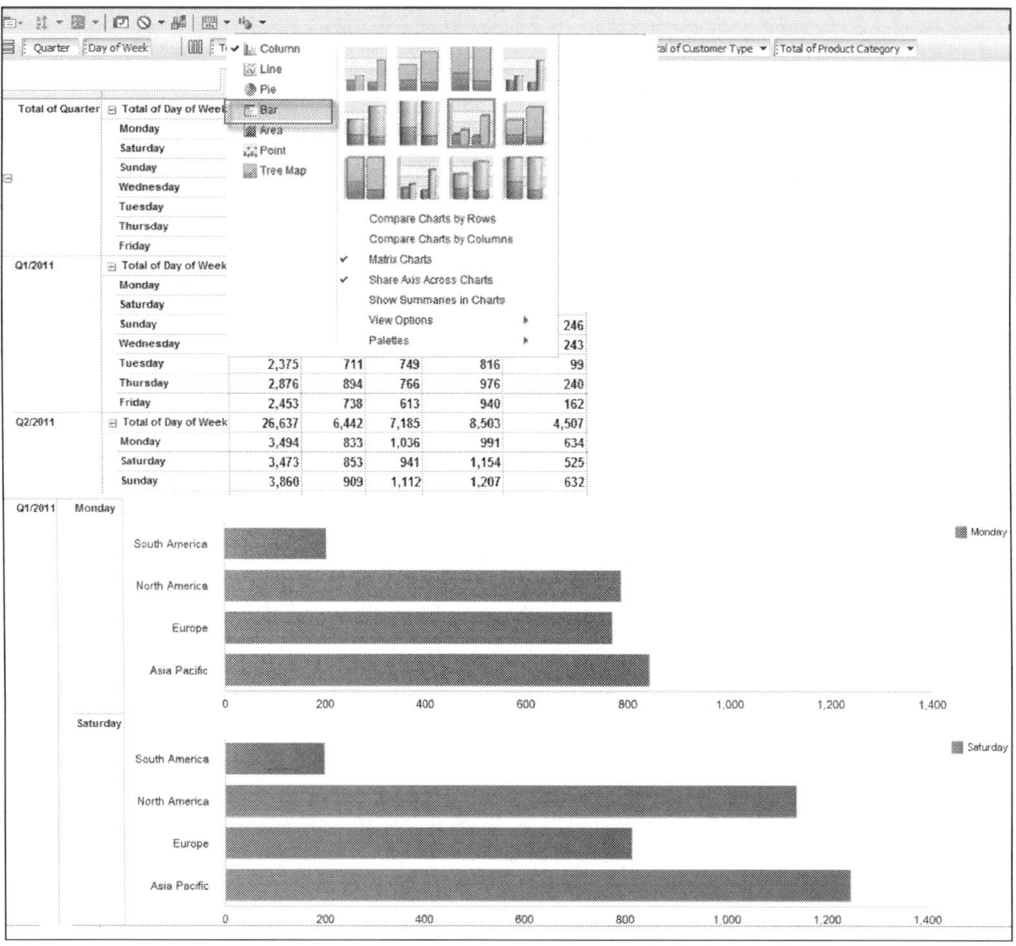

Filtering values/explorer points

The concept of explorer points in Cognos Insight enables filtering across multiple widgets in a workspace. From the content pane on the right-hand side, when dimensions are dragged onto the canvas area of the workspace, an explorer point for that dimension is created. Use the explorer points to filter the analysis and focus on areas of interest.

Resize the widget by restoring it using the restore icon to make room on the canvas for explorer points. Drag the **Territory** dimension onto the white space to create an explorer point for the **Territory** dimension as shown in the following screenshot:

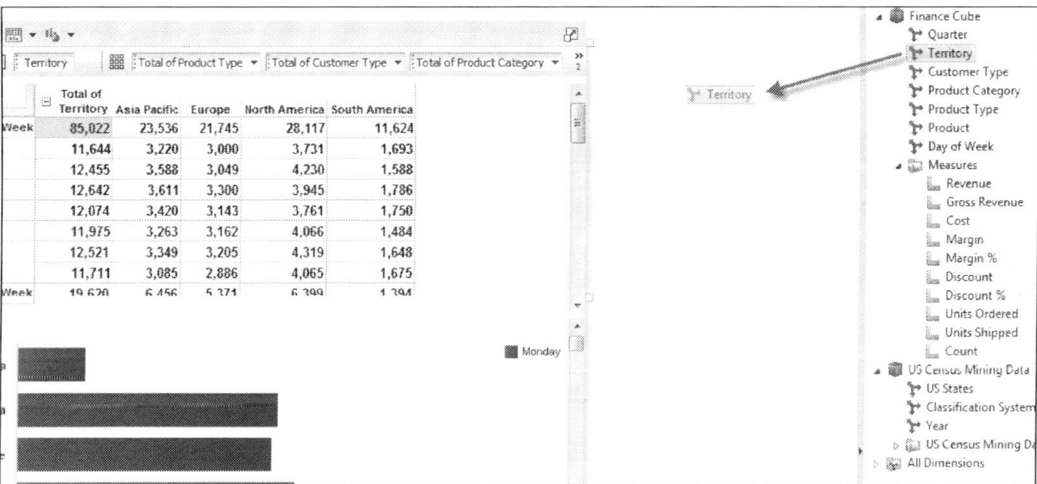

The following screenshot shows the explorer point for **Territory** dimension. The search icon on the top right-hand side of the explorer point enables us to search for data members within the dimension and is useful for large dimensions with many members. Clicking on the filter icon will disable the filter. The explorer point forms a widget on the canvas with its own properties and can be sized accordingly.

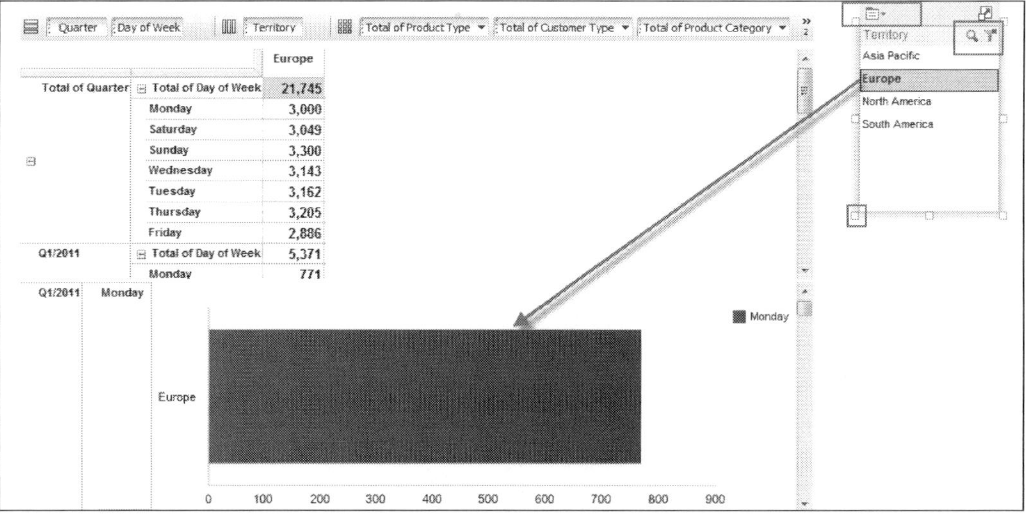

Additionally, Cognos Insight has the ability to display all the dimensions in an **Explore Pane**. Click on **Explore** in the title bar to see the **Explore Pane** on the left-hand side of the workspace. Other features such as disabling all filters or hiding the **Explore Pane** can be controlled from this drop-down as shown in the following screenshot:

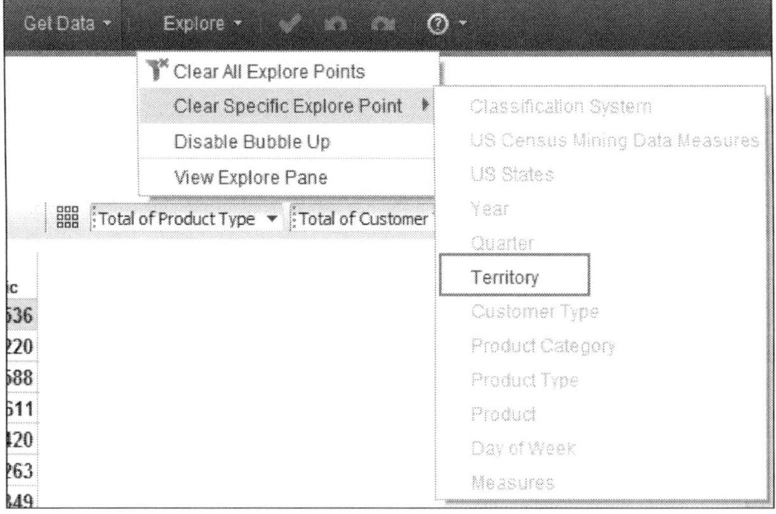

To make filtering easier with limited to no expression or coding required, Cognos Insight provides users to filter on top and bottom values. By selecting the column or row to filter, the menu driven option gives users the capability to filter on **Top or Bottom 3** to **5** or **10** data values or create custom ones, as shown in the following screenshot:

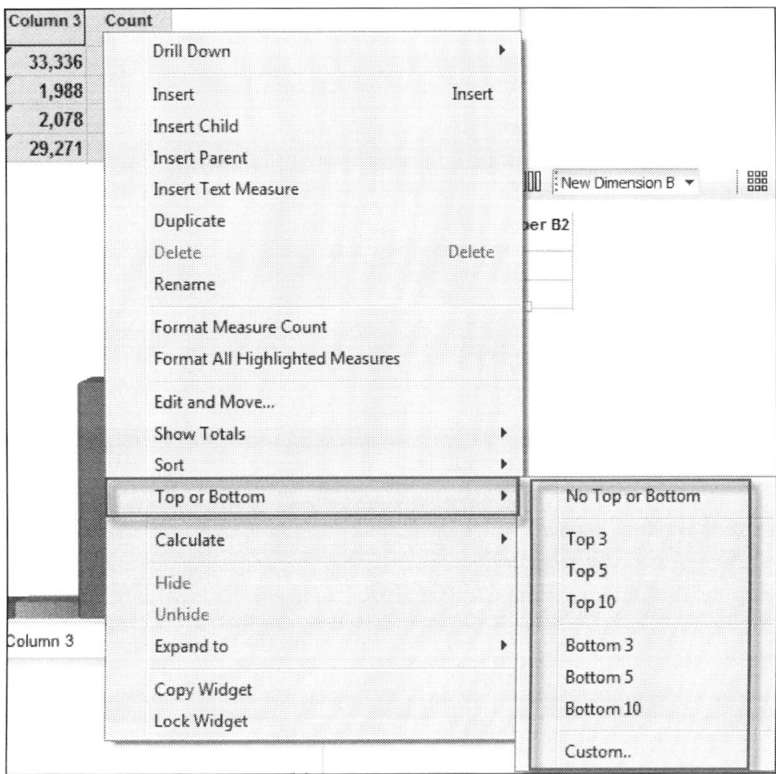

Types of calculations

Cognos Insight is capable of creating simple calculations such as additions, subtractions, multiplications, and divisions, and at the same time complex calculations involving comparative values to spot trends and discover sweet spots. As an example of a simple calculation, let's divide **Annual Payroll** by **No of All Workers** to see each worker's compensation.

As shown in the following screenshot, select the two column headers, right-click on them, and use the **Calculate** option to create a new calculated column:

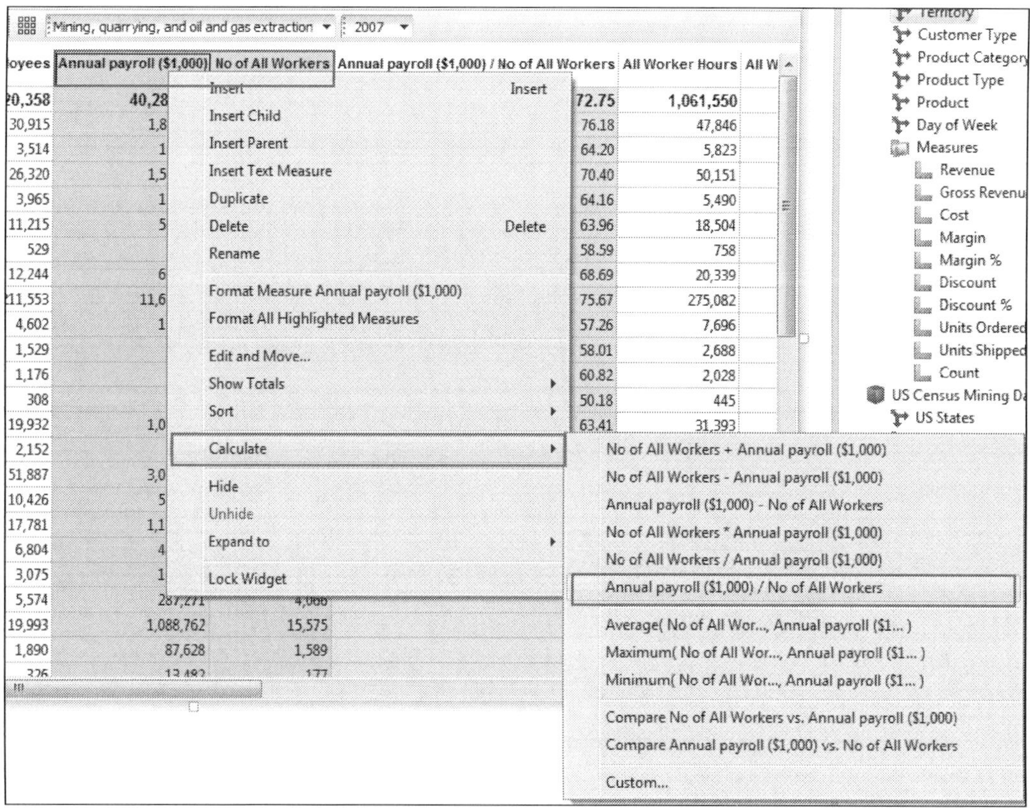

Another method of viewing the variance between the two columns or rows can be done by using the comparing values feature. In the following example, select the values, right-click and compare between *Texas and California* and *California and Texas*:

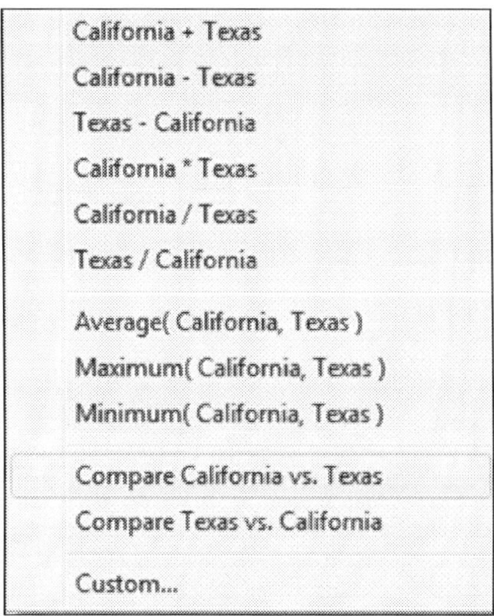

As shown in the following screenshot, a score card visual view of the variances is displayed. The metrics show the comparative values by a set of circles, squares, and diamond shaped objects.

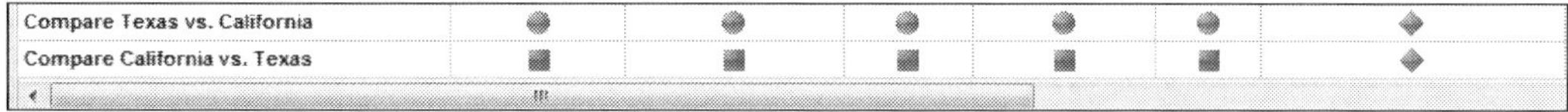

The score cards provide a new calculation metric. The green circle shows excellent values or 10 percent higher values than the comparative option, while the yellow diamond shows an average value, and the red square displays a 10 percent lower comparison, suggesting a poor variance change.

Creating customized or complex calculations in Cognos Insight can be accomplished by using calculation expressions. Each widget has a calculate icon which brings up the calculation expression window.

As shown in the following screenshot, the expression window has a calculation which will be executed specific to this cube/widget:

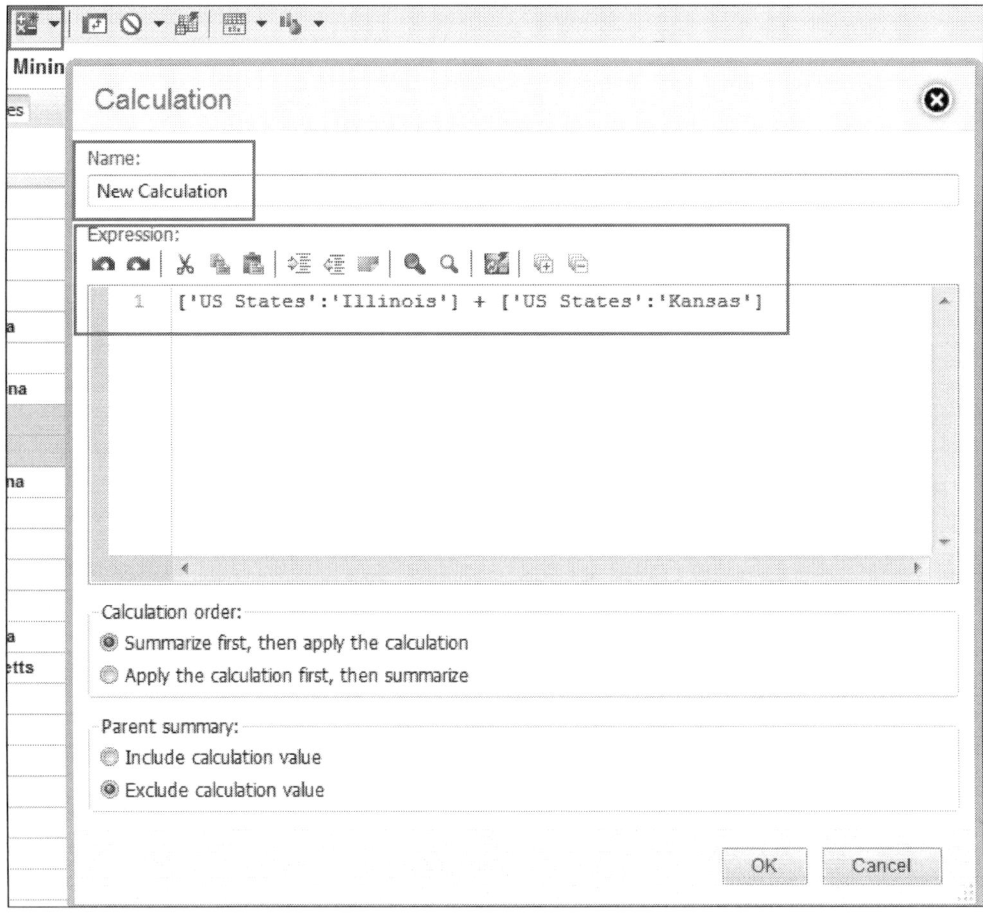

Some complex calculations would include gross margin percentage, profitability percentage, inventory turns, net present value, internal rate of return, return on invested capital, contribution values to totals, and so on.

Cognos Insight offers prebuilt **Rollup** for summaries such as **Average**, **Minimum**, **Maximum**, and **Count**, as shown in the following screenshot:

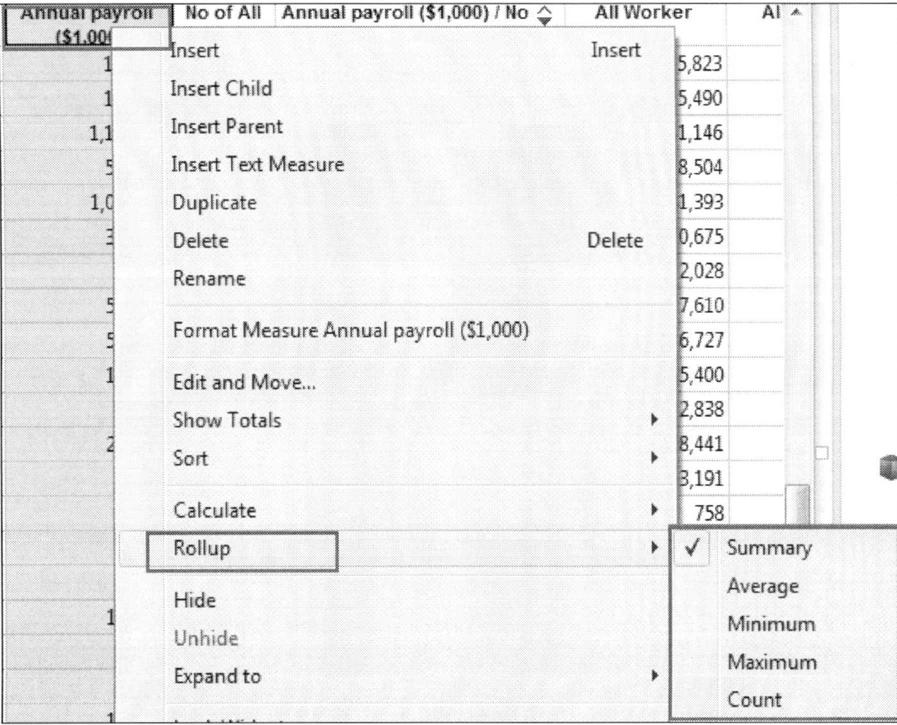

Editing calculations can be done by right-clicking on the new calculation and selecting **Edit this Calculation**. Alternatively, this can be done from the **Calculation** icon on the widget as well.

Writing rules

Adding complex calculations or business rules that are governed by complex calculated values, including cell level modifications, can be computed by writing rules in Cognos Insight. Like calculations, rules are written in the **Calculation** window and must end with a semicolon (;) as shown in the following screenshot:

Cube Rules - uscensusminingdata

Finance Cube   US Census Mining Data

```
 1   SKIPCHECK;
 2   UNDEFVALS;
 3   ['US States':'Compare California vs. Texas'] = IF(['US States':'California'] < ['US States':'Texas
 4       -1,
 5       IF(['US States':'California'] > ['US States':'Texas']*1.1,
 6           1,
 7           0
 8       )
 9   );
10   ['US States':'Compare Texas vs. California'] = IF(['US States':'Texas'] < ['US States':'California
11       -1,
12       IF(['US States':'Texas'] > ['US States':'California']*1.1,
13           1,
14           0
15       )
16   );
17   ['US Census Mining Data Measures':'Annual payroll ($1,000) / No of All Workers'] = ['US Census Mi
18   FEEDERS;
19   ['US Census Mining Data Measures':{'Annual payroll ($1,000)','No of All Workers'}] => ['US Census
20   ['US States':{'Texas', 'California'}] => ['US States':'Compare Texas vs. California'];
21   ['US States':{'California', 'Texas'}] => ['US States':'Compare California vs. Texas'];
```

As rules are cube specific, they can be accessed from the "widget actions" icon on the canvas of the workspace. Selecting the **Rules** option brings up the expression window.

In the previous screenshot, the highlighted keywords are the special functions used to compile rules in Cognos Insight. The expressions show all the calculations performed on this data set so far, which demonstrates that rules would have been written and complied with to accomplish the same calculations as done previously.

Formatting methods

Formatting data types to give more meaningful expressions can be done by selecting the options (right-click) on the measure header title or cell and selecting **Format measure-name**. This will open a new formatting window as shown in the following screenshot:

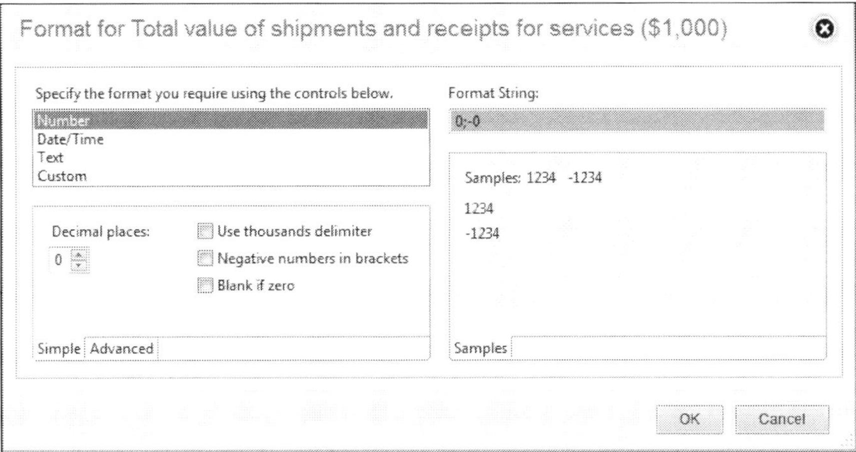

Use this window to apply **Currency values**, **Date**, and **Text** formats and a flexible **Custom** format.

Alternatively, the same formatting window can be accessed by selecting **Edit and Move** on each row or column header (right click). To modify the formatting changes, use the right-hand side of the window to apply the changes, as shown in the following screenshot:

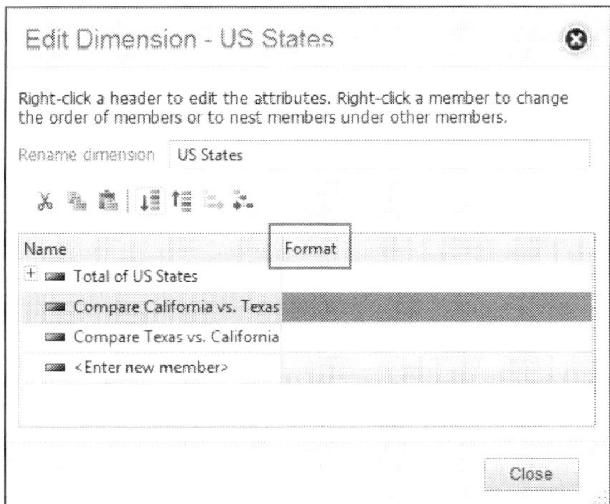

Grouping dimensions

One of the features in Cognos Insight used to display data in a structured format is by grouping dimensions. Grouping dimensions makes it easier to navigate across dimensions and is a cube specific feature. Adjust the dimension structure by using the wizard that is available from the content pane cube option (right click), as shown in the following screenshot:

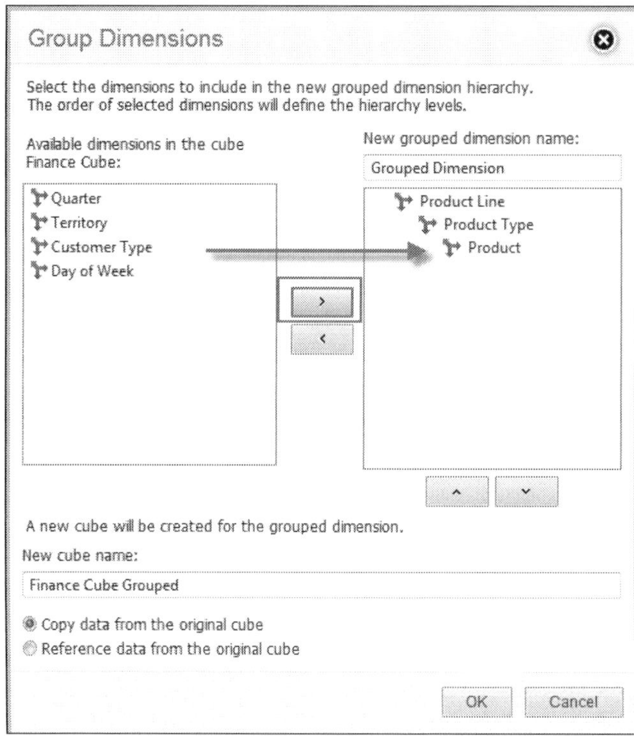

Once the dimensions to be grouped have been moved from the left-hand side to the right-hand side in the order of grouping or forming hierarchy, provide a name for the new cube that will be created for this. Use the available options in the wizard to either reference or copy the data from the original cube.

Reconstructing data in Cognos Insight

As an analytical tool that resides over data, Cognos Insight provides users with the ability to create what-if scenarios in a personalized sandbox environment, which can then be pushed towards a contribution. Added flexibility allows users to continue contributing to plans while being in connected or distributed mode, as well as offline mode. Users that are offline can continue to work on their plans and sync up their contributions once back online. With some restrictions towards data structural changes, this is a fairly seamless process. Cognos Insight also allows for the creation of OLAP components such as dimensions, measures, and members within the application itself in cases when the imported raw data lacks the needs to complete an analysis.

This section will describe the various features used to reconstruct data and use spreading techniques to accomplish the what-if scenario analysis. These features are as follows:

- Write-back
- Data spreading
- Adding cubes, dimensions, and members
- Adding parent and child members
- Moving members
- Adding comments

Write-back

Write-backs are used for what-if scenario planning. This allows analyst users to create business scenarios for planning and forecasting purposes. These could be used to generate a demand plan or forecast depending on the kind of data and how it is utilized.

Cognos Insight is built on IBM TM1 (OLAP) technology, and much like TM1 Cubes, Cognos Insight stores data at the lowest level cells. For example, with time dimensions having levels from year to day, data is stored at the day level and all calculations and summarizations are performed on the fly (in memory). This is the reason for the performance improvement in TM1 and Cognos Insight as compared to other OLAP applications on the market.

When performing write-backs at a higher level, all the lower level cells that are related to the range of write-backs get affected. After a write-back is performed and the values change, the font color changes from default black to blue, indicating cells or ranges within the data set that are affected by the write-back. These newly changed values are only written back to the TM1 (cube) database, when the user (administrator only) making the changes **commits** to the new values. Once a commit is done, as shown in the following screenshot, the font changes back to default black and all the changes made by the user are applied to the entire workgroup.

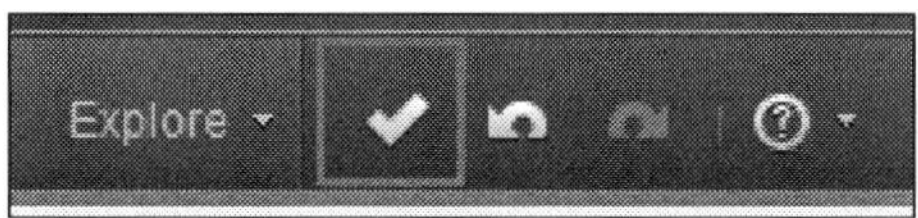

The personal sandbox environment now publishes the changes to an environment where all users will see the new changes. The same concept works with deleting items in the workspace. As soon as a commit is performed, all users are affected by the change. Hence, to better manage these situations, a strict governance and workflow process may be applied to audit data changes and track accountability amongst the user base.

As an example of the use case for write-back functionality, analysts are tracking the effects of a probable increase in the cost of manufacturing products in Europe based on current global trends. To forecast this event, an increased value of $2 million is added on to the existing $68 million to see the effects across Total Territory.

In the following example, typing **70M** in the highlighted cell will write-back 70,000,000 and apply it towards the entire analysis. Once applied, notice the blue fonts representing all affected cells and regions:

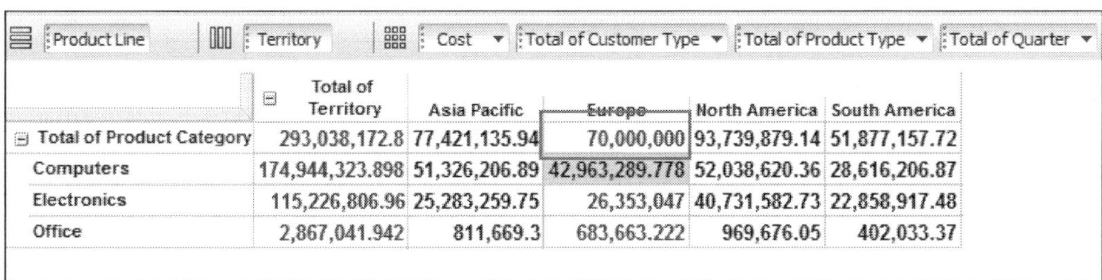

	Total of Territory	Asia Pacific	Europe	North America	South America
Total of Product Category	293,038,172.8	77,421,135.94	70,000,000	93,739,879.14	51,877,157.72
Computers	174,944,323.898	51,326,206.89	42,963,289.778	52,038,620.36	28,616,206.87
Electronics	115,226,806.96	25,283,259.75	26,353,047	40,731,582.73	22,858,917.48
Office	2,867,041.942	811,669.3	683,663.222	969,676.05	402,033.37

This shows the overall costs associated with the increase and how it affects the various products within the region. The what-if planning using Cognos Insight provides readiness and gives deeper insight into future decision making. This proves to be a valuable feature not only in volatile market conditions but also in planning, forecasting, and budgeting more accurately across all industry domains.

Cognos Insight has shortcuts available for write-backs such as "grow", "hold", and "^", which translates to increased values, hold cell values, and copy data values to all the children, respectively.

Applying **Hold** on a cell or group of cells will lock their values and prevent these locked cells from being affected by any write-backs or data spreading.

If a cell or group of cells have a hold, select the cell or area of cells and release the hold (right-click) as shown in the following screenshot:

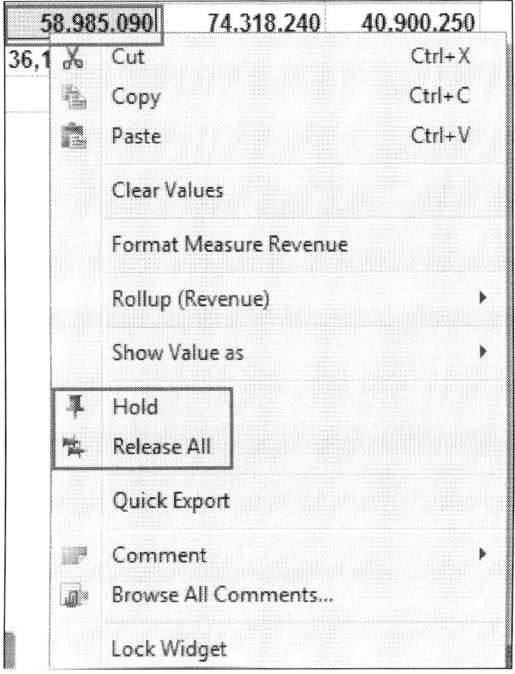

In Cognos Insight, what-if scenarios can be applied directly on graphs as well. Click on the **Revenue** measure for the **Office** product category and drag the cell upwards to show increase in revenue. As shown in the following screenshot, this has the same effect as the write-backs performed on crosstabs.

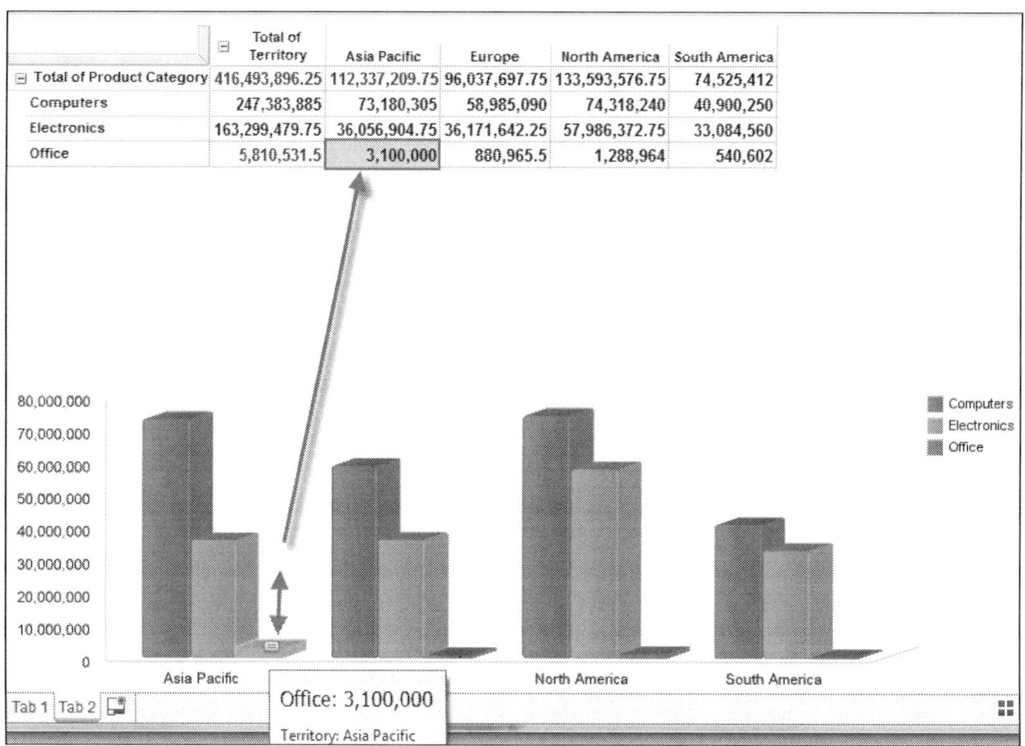

Data spreading

Data spreading is a technique used by analysts to spread numbers or values across regions of cells. This is typically used for modifying numbers using predefined or custom techniques such as **Equal Spread** and **Relative Proportional Spread**. In Cognos Insight, selecting on the aggregate cell to spread data brings up the data spread wizard. **Equal Spread** will spread values equally among all selected cells. If 1000 is input across an area of 10 cells, the value 100 will be distributed into each cell.

Relative Proportional Spread spreads the desired value based on the numeric values of the selected or reference cells. This can be based on other dimensions such as time or region to provide complex data distribution techniques, as shown in the following screenshot:

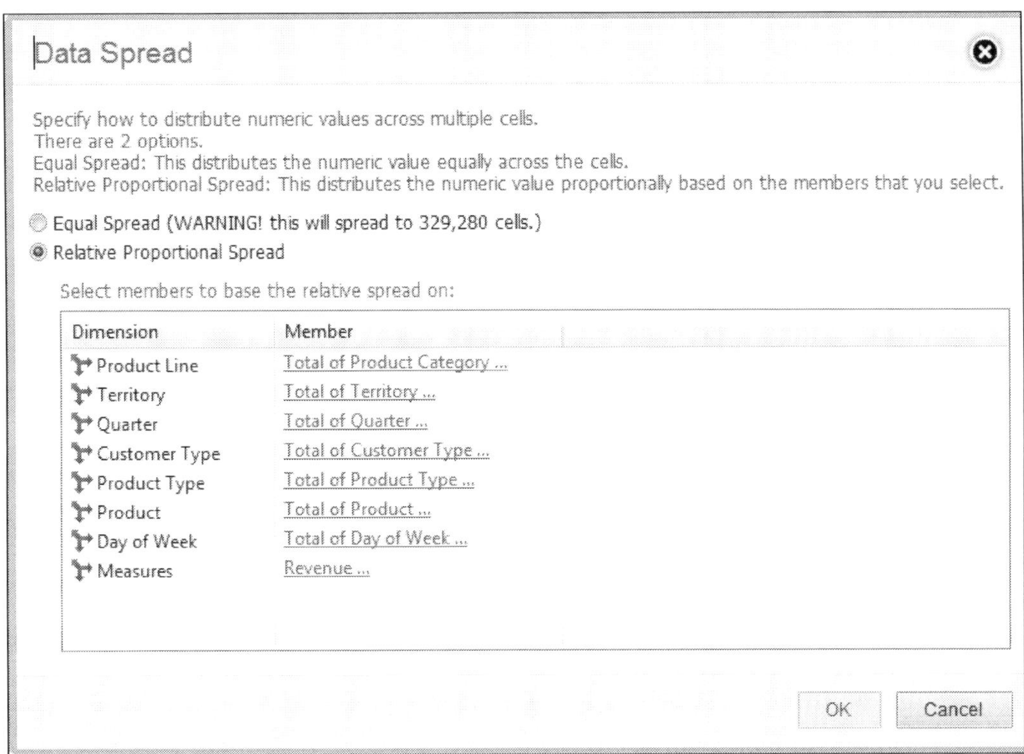

Adding cubes, dimensions, and members

These simple methods will assist in creating cubes and dimensions for additional analysis. Creating cubes and dimensions in Cognos Insight will allow users to input data into the new cubes manually, by data spreading techniques or by copy-pasting values directly into it. This can be done from the content pane on the right-hand side of the workspace where the **New** icon, as shown in the following screenshot, will create a **Blank Cube**.

This functionality provides users with the flexibility to bring in new data into their analysis. As mentioned previously, this data can be input manually or by other means. The addition of cubes can be used to enhance data sets and dashboards or for creating calculations and rules that rely on this new data rich cube.

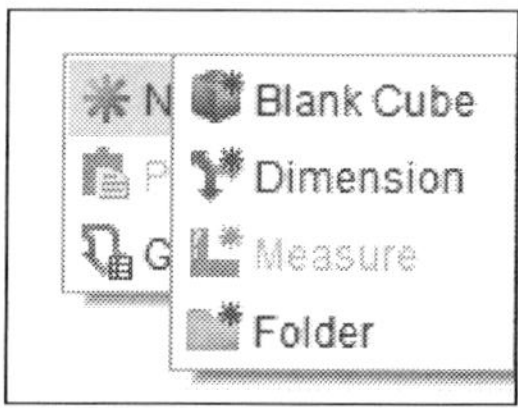

This will create a simple blank data cube with two dimensions and one measure within a measure folder as shown in the following screenshot:

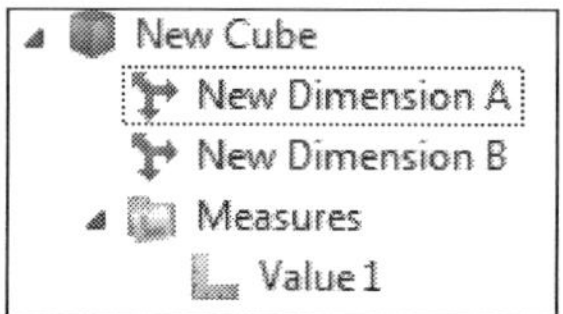

Similarly, add dimensions to the existing cubes and measures as well. The measures and cubes can be stored in folders for organization purposes. The addition of **Dimensions** can be done as shown in the following screenshot:

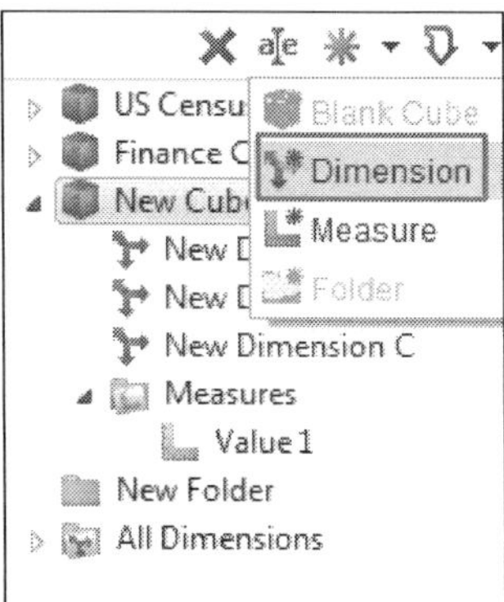

The addition of **Measures** can be done as shown in the following screenshot:

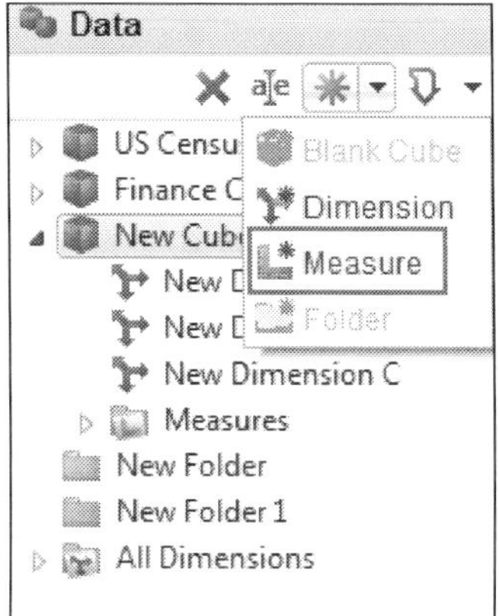

The creation of folders can be done as shown in the following screenshot:

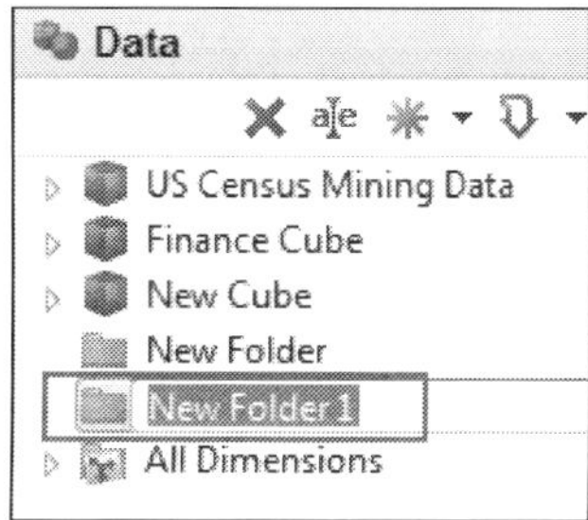

Another method of adding a cube to a workspace within Cognos Insight is by leveraging the **Insert** menu on the tool bar, as shown in the following screenshot:

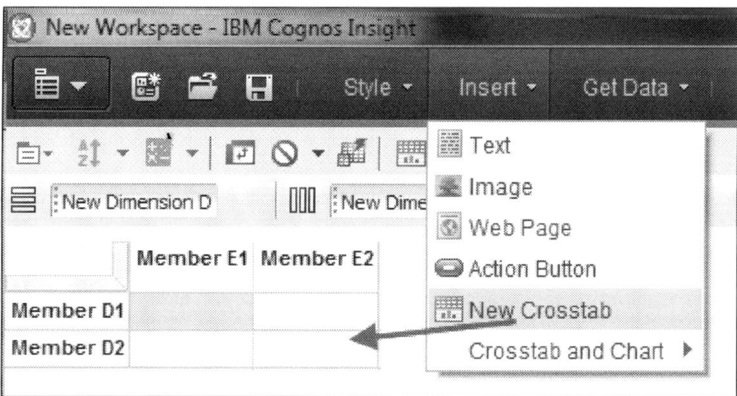

Sharing and reusing dimensions in a Cognos Insight workspace can save tremendous amounts of time in development efforts. Within Cognos Insight, dimensions can be copied or shared from one cube and used in another using the drag-and-drop method. This is followed by a wizard that assists with the process and can be seen in the following screenshot:

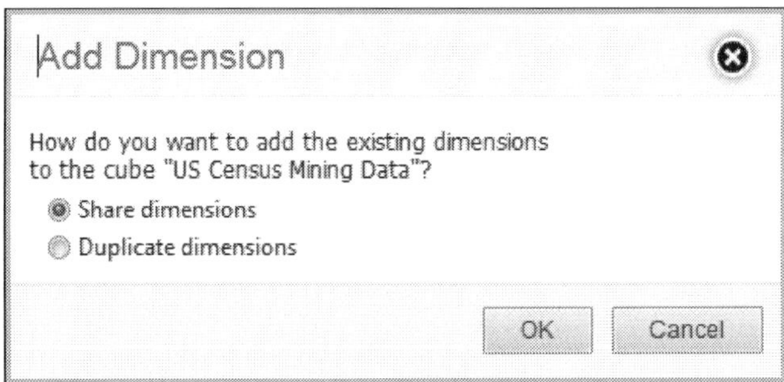

Adding parent and child members

Additional flexibility allows users to add data items within a cube and modify the structure of the cubes. As shown in the following screenshot, adding data items to existing data elements within a dimension such as the **Regions** dimension enables children and parent members to be added. Here, a data element such as the city **Dallas** can be added as a data child element to **Texas**. Similarly, a parent element can be added such as **US States** to which **Texas** becomes a child.

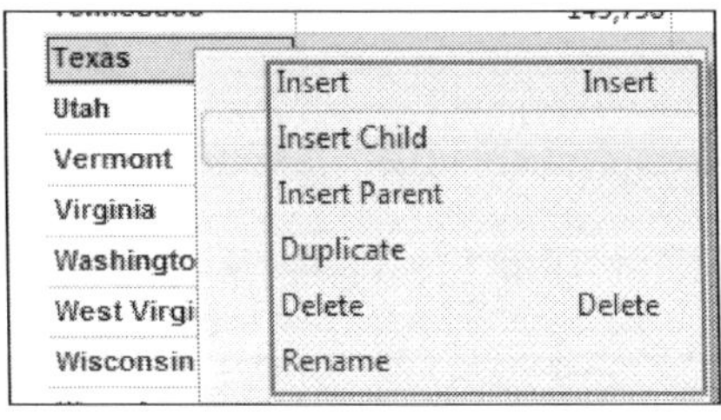

In the following example, **Dallas** is added as a child level into the **US State** of **Texas**.

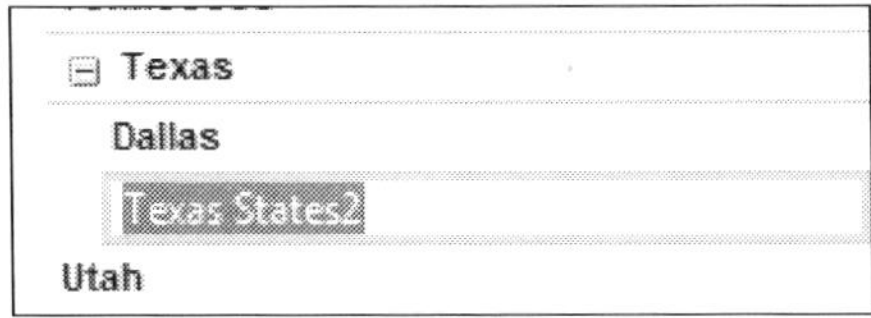

To **Delete**, **Rename**, or **Duplicate** a member, make the appropriate selection from the list as shown in the previous screenshot.

Moving members

Users can overwrite the order of elements in a dimension by using the **Edit and Move** feature in Cognos Insight to move members within a dimension, as shown in the following screenshot where **Texas** is added before **Tennessee** in the regions dimension using the drag-and-drop functionality:

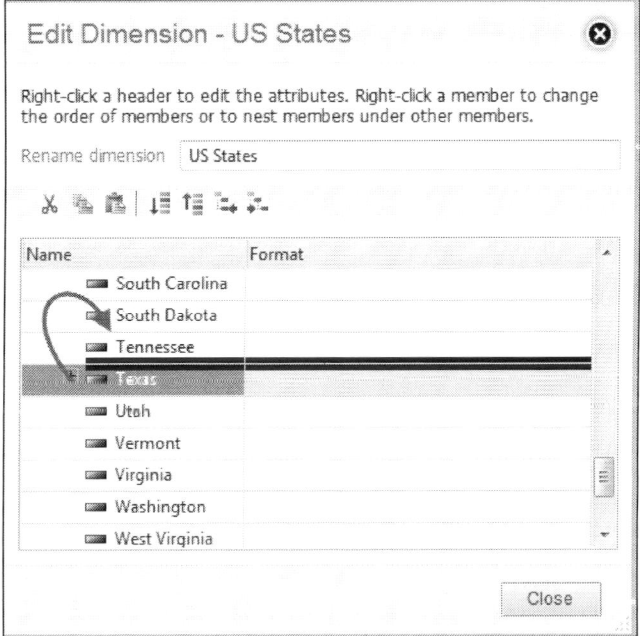

Adding comments

Comments are useful when doing analysis and what-if scenario planning to leave notes. This is particularly useful for financial analysts or anyone dealing with critical data. Cognos Insight has the ability to apply comments on individual cells so users can modify changes and write justifications for doing so as per their business requirements. The comments are stored and can be extracted for auditing purposes. A comment can be applied to a cell as shown in the following screenshot:

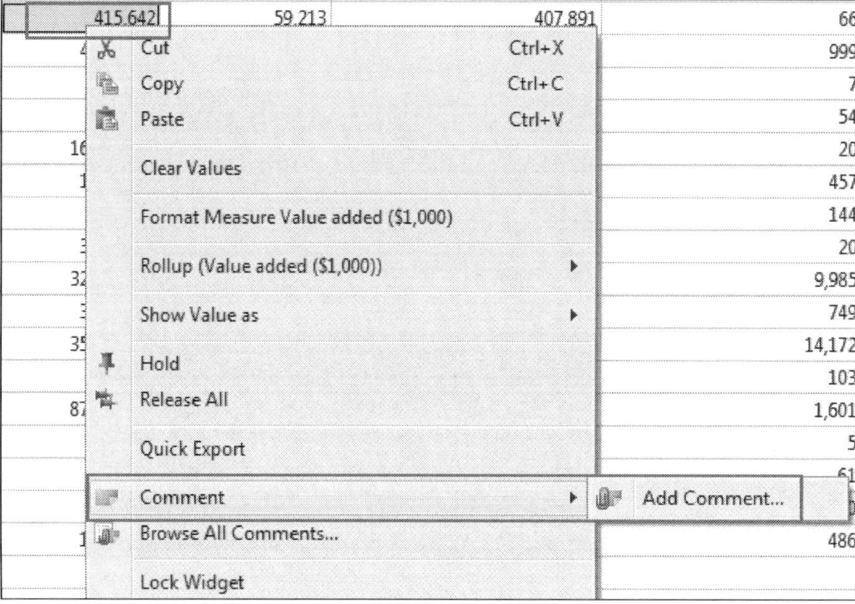

Additional functionality using **Browse All Comments...** displays all comments. These can also be deleted based on the user's request.

Cosmetic changes to Cognos Insight

By this point, most of the usability features of Cognos Insight have been discussed. The remaining features, listed as follows, will enhance the look and feel of the Cognos Insight workspace:

- Adding widgets, charts, and tabs
- Adding images, buttons, and themes
- Zero suppress and exporting data
- Protecting workspaces and my preferences

Adding widgets, charts, and tabs

Cognos Insight has no documented limits as to how many tabs and widgets can be added to a workspace. However, for clarity and data digestion it is recommended to build dashboards that are clean and provide a concise amount of information. This introduces adding multiple widgets and tabs to a workspace. The following screenshot shows adding a new cube to the workspace as it acts as a data container for a new widget:

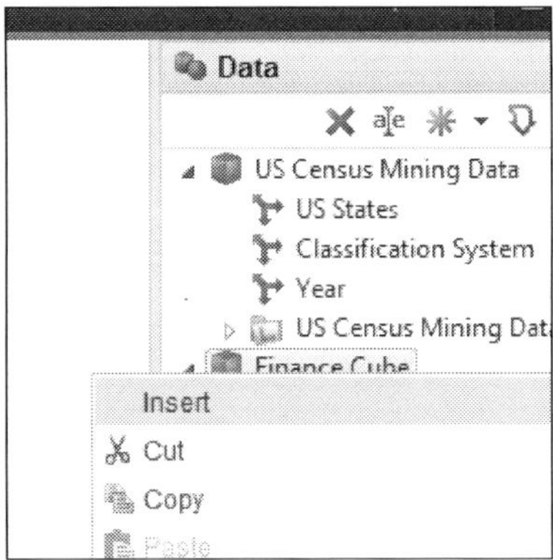

Each of the multiple widgets on a canvas have their own settings that make the widget unique. The following screenshot displays the list of available options:

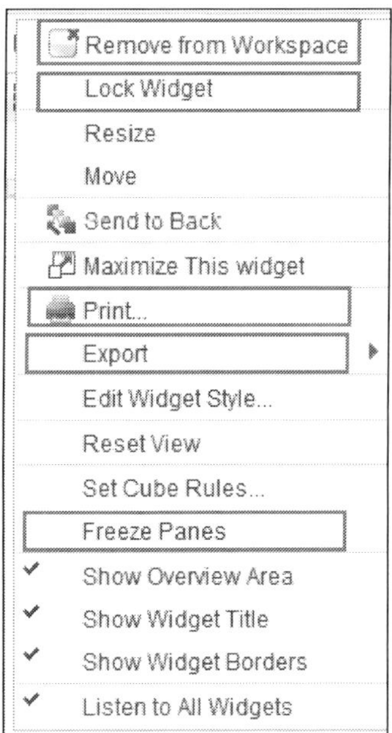

A list of available options and the description of each option is shown in the following table. Use the **Lock Widget** feature to avoid moving around the widgets and apply **Freeze Panes** when necessary.

Options	Description
Remove from Workspace	This removes the widget from the canvas area of the workspace.
Lock Widget	This helps to lock the widget when ready to share the workspace or avoid accidentally moving around the widgets.
Print	This option prints widgets to a printer. A printing wizard asks for the items to include in each tab.
Export	This option imports the widget either to an Excel spreadsheet or CSV file.
Freeze Panes	This option freezes the pane to enable scrolling across rows or columns without losing sight of critical headings.

Add tabs by selecting the add icon next to each tab on the bottom left-hand side of the workspace, as shown in the following screenshot:

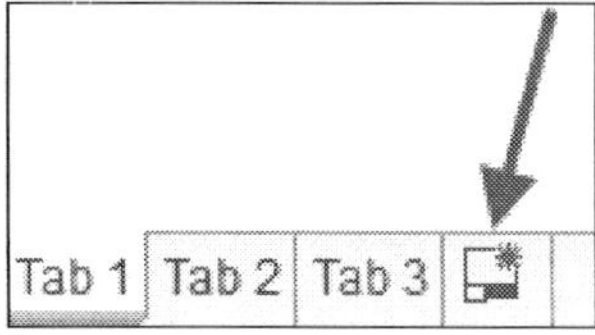

Use multi-tab workspace files to store more data, cubes, and widgets. As the data resides within Cognos Insight (unless in server connected mode), the more tabs and cubes per workspace, the larger the files tend to be.

Adding images, buttons, and themes

Images, text items, buttons, and themes add cosmetics and usability to workspace files. As shown in the following screenshot, leverage the **Insert** menu on the toolbar to bring each of these items onto the canvas:

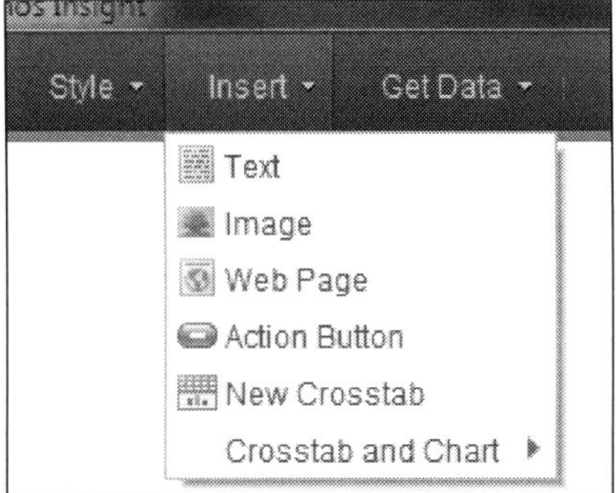

Adding text items such as dashboard title or widget/area title can be done and placed anywhere on the workspace canvas by double-clicking on the canvas area. As shown in the following screenshot, this brings up a textbox with formatting options:

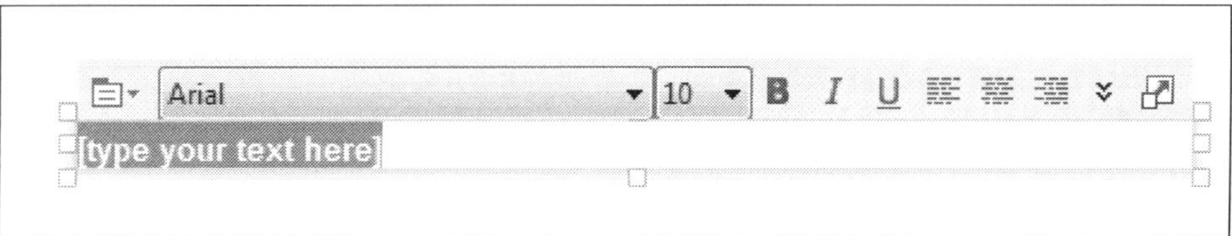

Action buttons are very useful and can serve two purposes:

- It can provide a navigation technique to go from one tab to another when dealing with multi-tab workspaces.

- It can run a TM1 "TurboIntegrator" script. This script can be used for refreshing data for the cube or for any other purpose as set by the TM1 administrator.

The following screenshot shows the properties of the **Action** button. Images can be used as buttons and styles can also be applied to the action button to enhance the look of the workspace.

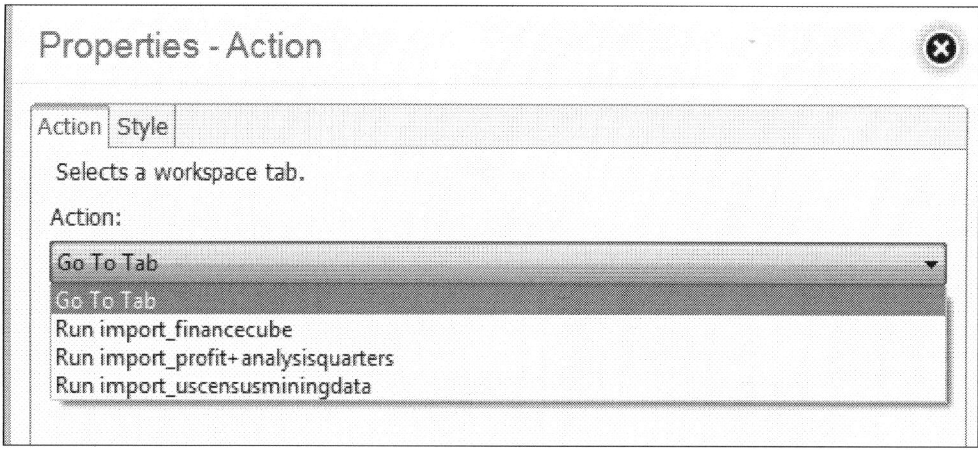

Cognos Insight has pre-defined themes that give a visual appeal to the canvas and workspace. Custom themes can also be created based on the user's preferences that include logos or corporate color codes. Use **Style** on the menu tool bar to apply a predefined theme as shown in the following screenshot:

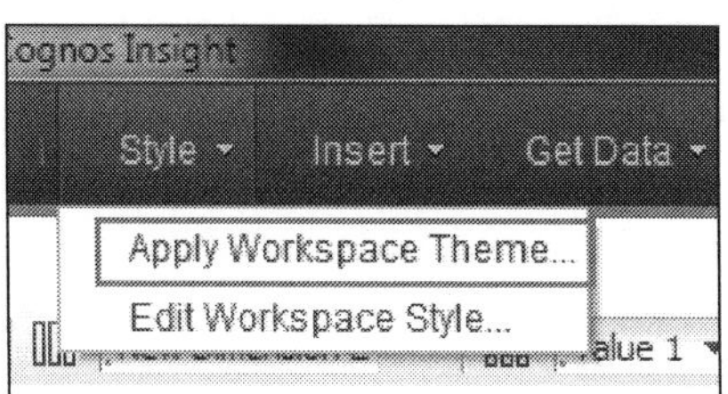

The following screenshot shows the **Focus** theme used on an existing workspace:

	Revenue	Gross Revenue	Cost	Margin	Margin %	Discount	Discount %	Units Ordered	Units Shipped
Total of Quarter	0	420,448,450	293,038,172.8	124,309,137.1	1,430.474	5,948,782.25	76.098	80,517	90,022
Q1/2011	0	107,426,850	75,099,528.601	31,528,373.72	466.452	1,710,417.75	28.056	22,326	20,774
Q2/2011	0	150,442,075	104,736,734.756	44,817,583.34	451.307	1,836,783.5	20.537	25,752	28,203
Q3/2011	0	132,972,075	92,609,337.164	39,134,471.24	378.76	2,061,211	21.707	25,180	25,956
Q4/2011	0	29,607,450	20,592,572.279	8,828,708.8	133.956	340,370	5.798	7,259	15,089

Zero suppress and exporting data

Another feature that can be used to present clean and concise data is that of zero suppression. In Cognos Insight, apply this feature for each widget to suppress the zero values on rows or columns as shown in the following screenshot:

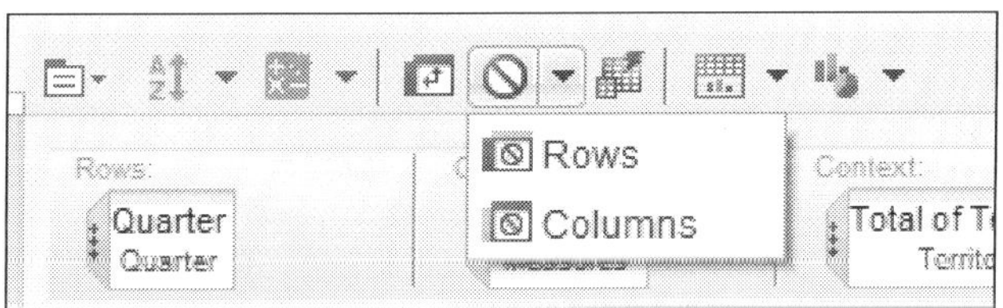

A usability feature that will save a tremendous amount of time is the exporting of cube data to CSV files. All development efforts applied to a workspace, including calculations, rules, formatted cells, and more, can be sent out to a CSV file by using the **Export to CSV** feature as shown in the following screenshot. This will export the data to a user selected location.

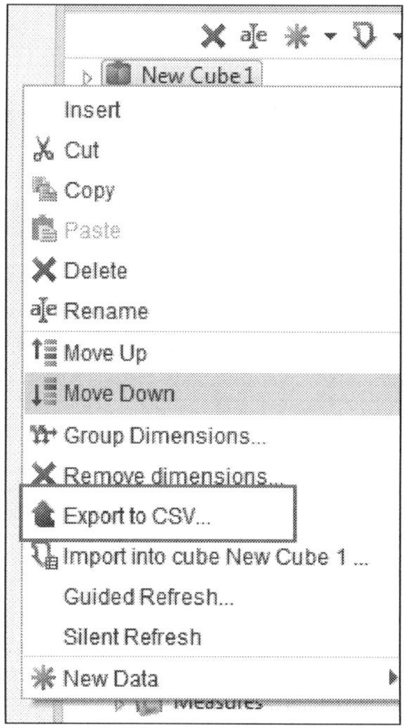

Protecting workspaces and my preferences

As described in *Chapter 2, Installing IBM Cognos Insight*, workspaces can be shared with other users of Cognos Insight. Whether sending workspaces across private/public networks or publishing them to Cognos Business Intelligence, Cognos Express, or IBM TM1 environments, protecting workspace files (cdd extension) is always a good practice. The **Actions** menu on the top left-hand side corner of Cognos Insight provides the means to password protect workspaces, as shown in the following screenshot:

As a recommendation, when using Cognos Insight to publish workspaces to enterprise wide environments, use the **My Preference** menu option under **Actions** menu. As a one-time action, this will set the parameters needed to connect to other IBM applications such as the Cognos Business Intelligence portal, Cognos Express, IBM Business Viewpoint, or IBM TM1. Once the necessary parameters are authenticated, sharing and publishing data is defined. Some of the preferences are shown in the following screenshot:

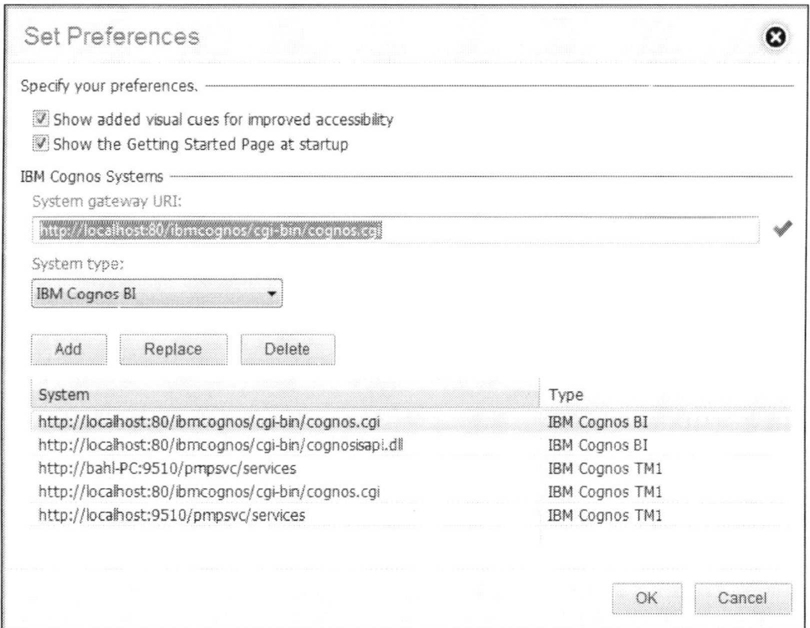

Summary

After installing Cognos Insight, leveraging the functions of this application will help in building workspaces. This chapter showed the various features within Cognos Insight that enable users to be self-sufficient in building and publishing workspaces not just to enterprise environments but to also utilize this as a self-service desktop application. Learning about the various flexibilities that Cognos Insight provides opens the *field of creativity* for building workspaces to analyze data to analysts and developers. Visualizing data in multiple orientations and creating calculations along with rules only adds to the usability and options for customized requirements. The next chapter will focus on building analysis using IBM Cognos Insight workspaces to spot trends, better understand data, and build analyses with rich visual content.

4
Strategic Decision Making Using IBM Cognos Insight

The previous chapter demonstrated various features and functionalities of IBM Cognos Insight, describing in detail how and when to use some of them. In this chapter, we shall utilize our new knowledge of Cognos Insight for building workspaces, using its features to analyze data and make decisions. Let us begin this chapter with a scenario where a company is looking to outsource its marketing, sales, and future revenue generation capabilities to a fictitious company called **PointScore**. PointScore has established itself as a research firm that helps its clients in making decisions, based on the actual research data and plugging in predictive intelligence to build case studies to justify the investments and further development.

In this situation, the client is looking to develop and launch a set of new electronic video games worldwide and hires PointScore to provide the business analysis and investment justifications. PointScore will analyze global market conditions, demographics, advertising strategies, consumer sentiment, customer demands, develop sales strategies, and create various product pricing options. By intelligently analyzing this data, PointScore is looking to provide a justification of the investment to its client to launch a new product type outside its core competency (new to the business). The new product type hopes to align the strategic initiatives of the client to match the competitive markets and provide an entry point into a market share that has not been pursued yet. The goal for launching this new product type will also be to create an excitement within the employees of the company and enhance the corporate image.

To accomplish these objectives, PointScore has chosen IBM Cognos Insight and other IBM Cognos Business Analytics suites of products to analyze the research and present it to their client. The in-house analysis will be performed using Cognos Insight by various departments such as marketing, sales, and finance. This holistic approach is needed to minimize the time to market the new products, provide a sales direction and a pricing strategy. The cross-functional teams working to accomplish this project will import researched data into Cognos Insight and tie up the analysis together. Thereafter, Cognos Insight workspaces will be delivered to the client to present the objectives and outcomes that PointScore was assigned with.

Analyzing marketing conditions

Marketing departments define the face of a product or organization. The definition of a new product, service, or company depends on surveys and strategies from data analysis. Marketing for new products across a global audience requires deep insights into the global market conditions, customer needs, customer base, field of competition, and product information.

PointScore has researched this data and is now putting it together using IBM Cognos Insight to answer questions such as the following:

- How favorable are the global markets to launch the new product?
- What demographics make up our target customer base?
- How are our competitors performing in the same market?
- How can we best infiltrate the market using streamlined advertising strategies?

These and other marketing questions answered intelligently will prove to be critical in providing the go-ahead signal for the product marketing and the strategy to gain a market share of a new business venture.

The analysis will begin by understanding the end customer better. PointScore's R&D department provides a customer data spreadsheet that will act as the data source.

The following instructions will help build a Global Customer Survey analysis using Cognos Insight. Use the `Customer.xls` file provided with this book as the data source for this workspace. At the end of these instructions is the final output file, as seen in the screenshot that will follow:

1. Drag and drop the customers' data onto the Cognos Insight application.
2. Reorient the initial view of the data by dragging and dropping the dimensions.

3. Replace the **Customer Measures** dimension by the **Product Type** dimension.

   This view will now show the various age groups of the customers segmented as rows along with the three **Product Types**—**Educational**, **Strategic**, and **3-D Games**. The **3-D Games** is the new **Product Type** that PointScore is going to study and analyze.

4. From the **Customer Measures** dimension, slice to the **Sentiments** element member. This initial observation shows a keen interest in the customer base for a 3D video game series. This excitement would be seen as positive news for PointScore's client.

5. Resize the widget to appear on the left-hand side of the workspace.

6. From the widget properties uncheck the **Listen to all widgets** option. This step makes the widget into a standalone widget.

7. Drag and drop the customer cube from the content pane on the right-hand side to the workspace.

8. Resize the widget to appear on the bottom of the workspace.

9. Replace the **Customer Measures** dimension by the **Regions** dimension.

10. Swap rows and columns: the **Regions** dimension is now a rows while **Age Group** is a column.

11. Stack/nest the **Country** dimension to the right-hand side of the **Regions** dimension.

12. Reorient the visual to show **Count** as **Measure**.

13. Display only the **Chart** from the **Change Display** icon.

14. Change the **Chart** type to show the **3D column chart**.

15. Under **Change Chart**, choose the **Compare Chart by Rows** option and change **Palette** to **Dynamic**.

16. From the widget properties, uncheck the **Listen to all widgets** option.

The analysis shows a higher number of customers in the Asia-Pacific region in the age group of 19-27 followed by the American region. This helps in focusing marketing efforts towards the specific micro-segmented markets to achieve the targeted audience.

1. From the content pane, drag and drop the customer cube again and resize the widget.

2. **Product Type** is the row dimension while **Competitor** is the column dimension.

3. Slice to **Revenue** from the **Measure** dimension.

4. Change the **Chart** display type to be **3D Pie** and **Palette** to **Dynamic**.

5. Apply a theme to the canvas with the title **Global Customer Survey**.

This analysis reveals that the competitive market share in the 3D video games belongs to **ForceGT**, followed by **Maseotronic**, while **Tall Tower** has its concentration towards **Educational** game types. As shown in the following screenshot, the **Customer** information is presented in a dashboard style using Cognos Insight:

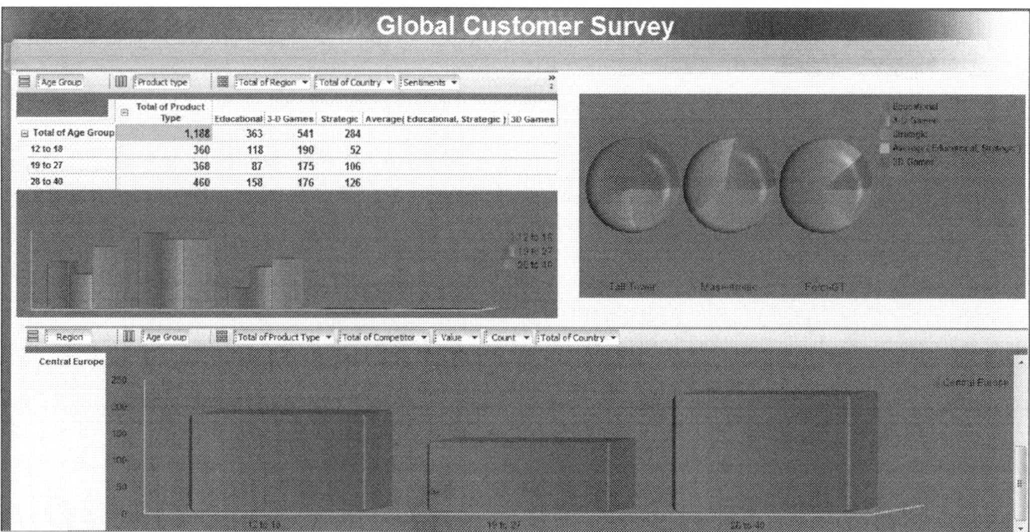

Advertising cost analysis

As a derivation of marketing analysis creating micro-segmented customer bases, advertising to the appropriate audience with the correlated material is essential. The analysis followed by the marketing department leads to the business' fixed cost expense, that is, advertising associated with the new product, the various channels, and their costs. These answers will give a better insight into the product cost and marketing methodology.

Some of the questions answered by marketing department through advertising would be:

- How much are we spending on advertising costs?

- Based on past experiences and factual data, what is the trend of spending for all the advertising costs?

- What is the average spending on all the advertising costs?

- Which method of advertising is returning more gains?

- How can we predict the outcome in spending costs for the new product type?

Let us apply the R&D department's researched data and utilize the spreadsheet in Cognos Insight as the data source, to analyze this data.

The following instructions will help build an advertising cost analysis using Cognos Insight. For this workspace, use the `AdvertisingCost.xls` spreadsheet as provided. At the end of these instructions is the final output file, as seen in the screenshot that will appear next:

1. Click to create a new tab in the existing Cognos Insight workspace.
2. Drag and drop the advertising data spreadsheet provided by the R&D department.
3. Reorient to have the **Advertising Measure** as the column dimension.
4. Swap the rows and columns.
5. *Ctrl*+click on select the **Revenue** and **Count** elements under the **Advertising Measures**.

As we are looking for the advertising costs, we can safely remove the **Revenue** and **Count** elements from the data analysis.

1. Drag **Year** in the column dimension to stack above **Product Type**.
2. Select **Educational** and **Strategic** members from the **Product Type** dimension.
3. Right-click on the selection and select **Calculation** to create an average of the two selections. This calculation will give an average of spending costs on advertising, based on the other two product types in the organization. This will be a predictive costs analysis based on historical trends followed by the client.
4. Hide any other columns or rows not required for the view. If there are other columns or rows that do not add value to the analysis other than what is in the scope, right-click on those items and select **Hide**.
5. Right-click on the newly-formed calculated column and select **Calculate** again.
6. From the given options select **Average * Number**.
7. Select **1.4** as the number to calculate. The **1.4** value suggests that the advertising costs across the board will be about **1.4** times the cost of the average spent for other product types per year. This details out the advertising expense costs by method.

8. Rename the new column to **3D Games**.

9. Hide the **First Average Calculated** column. This will keep the data view clean and concise. The idea is to get the fastest answers at a quick glance.

10. Right-click on the **Product Type** dimension and sort values by the descending method.

11. Add a title at the top of the workspace.

12. Add a text description with a summary of the analysis.

13. Lock all the widgets.

The following screenshot shows the advertising costs over the last two years. It also predicts the advertising costs related to the new product, based on the historical trends with respect to the other product types. Based on the visual dashboard, the overall advertising costs dropped compared to the previous year, but the write-back calculations suggest that the new product type will require slightly more investments.

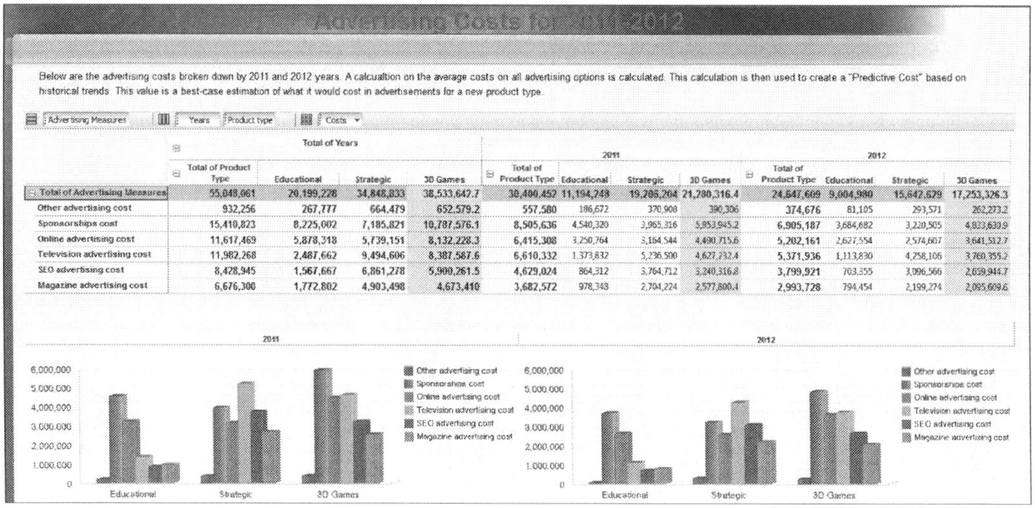

Product cost-benefit analysis

Given the financial investments poured into the R&D of a new product type development, PointScore has acquired financials of its client's other product types over the last two years. The intention is to leverage this data and the analytical capabilities of Cognos Insight to develop a fact-based probable revenue generation of the new product type—3D Games.

The result from this analysis will shed some light on the cost and benefits of launching this new product type into a mature market. Given the risks involved financially and the client's reputation at stake, a high level analysis followed by a detailed financial analysis of the clients sensitive data is performed to calculate product profitability. PointScore has been provided with a spreadsheet from the client's finance department, which has been passed on to PointScore's marketing head for further product analysis.

The following instructions will help build a Predictive Revenue analysis using Cognos Insight. Use the `Products.xls` spreadsheet as the data source to build this workspace. At the end of these instructions is the final output file as seen in the next screenshot:

1. Create a new tab and rename it to **Product Analysis**.

2. Drag and drop the **Products** spreadsheet file onto the worksheet.

3. With **Product Type** in the rows dimension, stack the **Year** dimension to the **Product Sales Measure** dimension. This measure dimension contains elements such as **Revenue** and **Production Cost**.

Next, a calculation needs to be added to calculate the ratio between the **Revenue** and **Production Cost**. An average of this ratio type can be used to predict the **Revenue** to be generated by the new product type.

1. *Ctrl*+click **Revenue** and **Production Cost** and right-click to select **Calculation**.

2. Create a calculation to find ratio of **Revenue/Production** Cost. A new calculated column is added to the analysis.

3. Select the row elements for **Education** and **Strategic**, right-click and select **Calculate**.

4. Create an average of the two selections.

A new row is added to the analysis. The intersection shows an average value of 1.206. This number is critical for the business analysis and is going to be used to determine future product revenue capabilities.

1. Resize the widget.

2. Insert a blank **Crosstab** into the current workspace.

3. Move this new widget to the right-hand side of the page.

4. Rename the new element row member to **3D Gaming**.

5. Rename the new element column member to **2013**.

6. Right-click on the **2013** member and select **Insert Child**.

7. Rename this column to **Production Cost**.

8. Type in the value of **4500**.

   This is a confidential value that has been provided by the client. This is a range of the **Production Cost** for the new product—3D gaming.

9. Right-click on the **Production Cost** column and create a calculation.

10. The new calculation should be a multiplication between **Production Cost** for **2013** and **1.206**.

11. Swap the rows and columns.

12. Change the chart type to be a 3D bar chart and an **Active Palette**.

13. Add a **Title Text** to the workspace.

14. Lock all the widgets.

As shown in the following screenshot, this analysis has quickly provided predictive revenue figures for the new product development. This revenue number is higher than the client's other two product types and is considered as a reinforcing go-ahead signal to be relayed to the client.

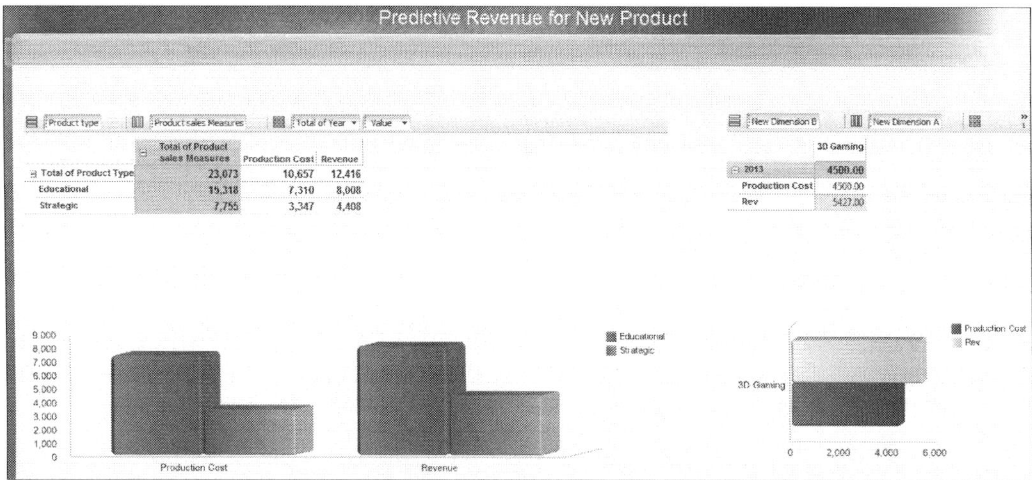

Global market conditions

With product, customer, and advertising costs defined and analyzed, PointScore researches Global Market trends to streamline strategic sales and marketing opportunities. This approach will provide the confidence and focus on markets where higher chances of sales with the launch of a new product exist. This high risk phase needs analysis, which will be performed using Cognos Insight to determine a priority of investments based on the analysis feedback and provide insight to maximize high returns in the first few weeks since the launch date.

The two measures used in this analysis are **Consumer Price Index (CPI)**, which measures the consumer confidence and the **Retail Sales**, which is used to analyze revenue from sales. Both of these measures will provide insight into the global trends among these regions and help in making better business decisions to favor the launch of the new products.

The following instructions will help build a Global Market Conditions analysis using Cognos Insight. Use the GMC.xls spreadsheet as the data source required to build the workspace. At the end of these instructions is the final output file as seen in the screenshot that will follow:

1. Create a new tab in the existing workspace and rename it to **Global Markets**.
2. Drag and drop the **GMC** researched spreadsheet file onto the new tab area.
3. **Regions** should represent the rows dimension and **Year** should represent the column dimension in the analysis.
4. Right-click on **Total of Year** and **Sort by Ascending (Sort by Label)**.
5. From the **Measure Dimension**, slice to select either **CPI** or **Retail Sales**.
6. Change the display chart to **Line** chart.
7. Resize the widget.
8. Drag and drop the **Regions** dimension to create an **Explorer Point** (filter).
9. Lock the widgets.
10. Add a **Title Text Item**.
11. Add a text summarizing the analysis.

As seen in the following screenshot, the analysis reveals that retail sales have fallen in Central Europe over the last 10 years and so has the consumer confidence. At the same time the American region has had an increase over the last 10 years. However, the increase is not as fast as the Asia-Pacific region.

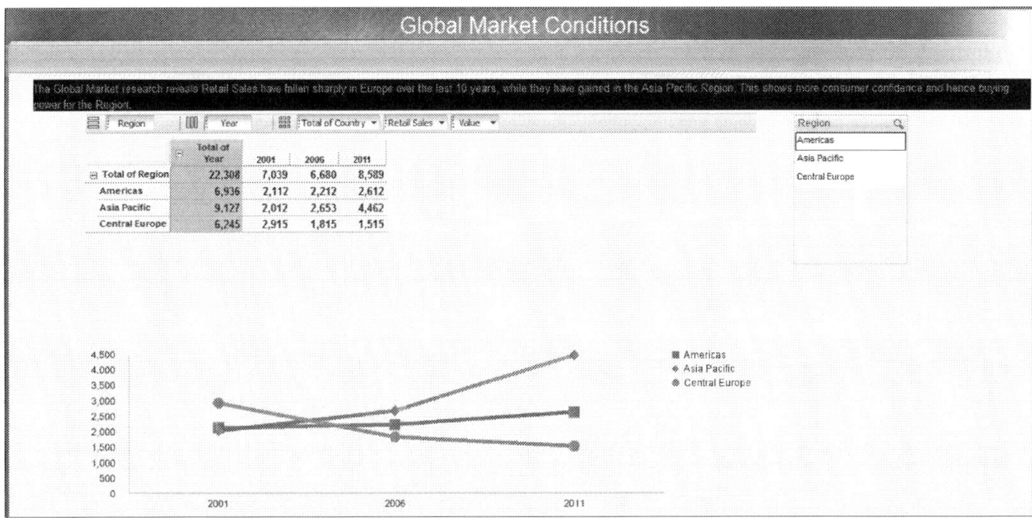

The Asia-Pacific region shows the highest retail sales and consumer confidence that leads to believe new products in this emerging market would pay off higher dividends than other regions. Hence to leverage this situation and maximize the regions' potential, it might be a good approach to launch the product in Asia prior to Central Europe.

With this, the marketing analysis has been completed. The analysis has revealed information about customer, product, advertising, and global markets—all the necessary domains when considering launching a new product.

Save this file as **Marketing Analysis**. The file or Cognos Insight workspace will have the extension `.cdd` and will contain all the TM1 cubes and the data used to build this analysis. This analysis can now be viewed offline as all the data resides on this file.

Measuring sales performance

To understand the revenue generation better, it is important to focus on sales. Better insight into the sales figures and an analysis on sales performance can enhance revenue streams for the company. Deeper sales analysis can enable companies to realize demand and plan supply.

PointScore is looking into the sales figures to find trends and better estimate sales by employees or "sales reps", and view sales by territory. This kind of analysis is done with the intention of using the historical data to plan for the future product release.

PointScore has obtained data from a similar situation from the year 2010, when its client launched another product type. Analyzing this data should answer questions such as the following:

- How are our employees performing?
- What are the sales reps' bonus structures and how is it affecting the performance?
- How are we performing across global territories?
- Which are the best sales quarters and why?
- How can we improve the sales pipeline and reduce returns?
- How many new customers are we selling to and how much revenue did our existing customers generate?

These and other questions can be answered with data analysis. PointScore is going to leverage Cognos Insight to answer these and other sales related questions for their client.

The following instructions will help build a sales performance by Employee and Region analysis using Cognos Insight. For this workspace, use the `ForSalesAnalysis.xls` spreadsheet as the data source. At the end of these instructions is the final output file as seen in the screenshot that will follow:

1. Drag and drop the **Sales Analysis** spreadsheet onto Cognos Insight.
2. Reorient the crosstab to show **Country** dimension in rows and **Sales Measures** in columns.
3. Create a **Variance** calculation between the **Actual** and **Target** columns.
4. Rename this column to **Variance**. This calculation will reveal the difference between the given target, based on budgets and growth, and the actual targets.
5. *Ctrl*+click the **Actual** and **Target** columns, right-click on **Compare Values**. Cognos Insight creates scorecard indicators based on data difference. This indicator is a visual to the **Variance** column and provides an 'at-a-glance' option into data. Predefined values set the three indicators based on the values **Excellent**, **Average**, and **Poor performance**.

6. Sort on **Variance** column by **Value** in the ascending order. The initial analysis shows **Australia** and **France** as the worst performing regions for the given year 2010, while **China** and **Canada** were the top performing territories.

7. Reorient the data to show the **Country** dimension as the row and **Territory** as the column.

8. Change the display type to **Chart** only.

9. Slice the **Measures Dimension** to the **Variance** data element. This analysis visually displays the sales performance of the territories and at-a-glance displays the top performers and bottom performers.

10. Resize the widget.

11. From the **Content** pane, drag the **Sales** cube onto the canvas.

12. Reorient to show the **Sales Rep** dimension as rows and **Measures** as column.

Sorting Variance columns in ascending order

To apply our focus on the lower performers, only show the rows of data that are the low five performers. The following are the steps to do this:

1. Select all the rows after **Jane Russell**, right-click, and select **Hide**.

2. Right-click on the **Actuals** column and select **Calculation**.

3. Select the option to multiply **Actuals** with **0.05**.

4. Create another calculation column to calculate a second bonus scenario based on 7.5 percent of **Actuals**.

5. Drag the **Country** dimension from the **Content** pane onto the canvas as an **Explorer Point** (filter).

6. Add a title to the page.

7. Lock all the widgets.

As seen in the following screenshot, the crosstab shows two scenarios of bonus figures for 7.5 percent and 5 percent. As the data focuses on sales reps who have not been up to the mark from the last time new products were developed, these two scenarios will be presented to the client as a sales bonus incentive. These incentives could be used to reward sales reps and by discussing their bonus rates could attract higher sales volume, thereby increasing sales for the region and the company.

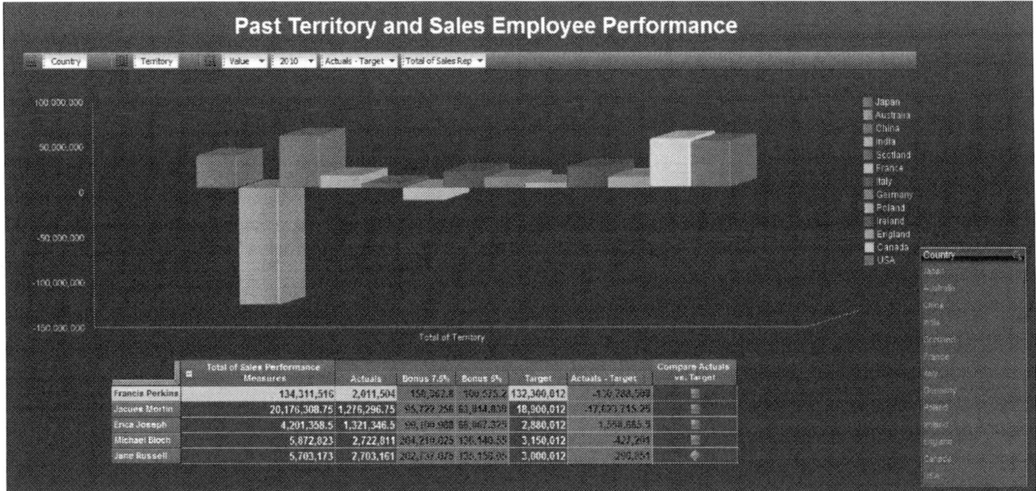

Total of Sales Performance Measures		Actuals	Bonus 7.5%	Bonus 5%	Target	Actuals - Target	Compare Actuals vs. Target
Francis Perkins	134,311,516	2,011,504	156,362.8	100,575.2	132,300,012	-129,288,508	
Jacque Mortin	20,176,308.75	1,276,296.75	95,722.256	63,814.838	18,900,012	-17,623,715.25	
Erica Joseph	4,201,358.5	1,321,346.5	99,100.988	66,067.325	2,880,012	1,558,685.5	
Michael Bloch	5,872,823	2,722,811	204,210.825	136,140.55	3,150,012	-427,201	
Jane Russell	5,703,173	2,703,161	202,737.075	135,156.05	3,000,012	290,851	

The following instructions will help build a Sales Variance analysis using Cognos Insight. For this analysis, leverage the sales cube from the earlier workspace. At the end of these instructions is the final output file as seen in the screenshot that will appear next:

1. Create a new tab and rename it to **Monthly Sales by Variance**.
2. Drag and drop the existing **Sales** cube from the content pane and resize the widget.
3. Reorient the data to show **Sales Performance Measures** as rows.
4. Show the **Month** dimension as columns.
5. Hide the **Quarterly** results from the columns.
6. In the rows, keep only **Actuals**, **Target**, **Actual-Target**, and **Compare Actuals vs. Target**.
7. Add an appropriate title to the page.
8. Lock all the widgets.

As seen in the following screenshot, the analysis reveals monthly sales figures for all the regions, by all employees, on a monthly basis. Taking into consideration an overall analysis, this shows that there was a considerable drop in **Variance** in the month of **November** and **December**.

Comparing these numbers to global economic conditions and being in a similar situation of new product development, this analysis is alarming for the 3D gaming product type. Sales executives would plan this as an opportunity and drive sales strategies, based on the poor performance in Q4, and analyze Q2 and Q3 as higher revenue quarters.

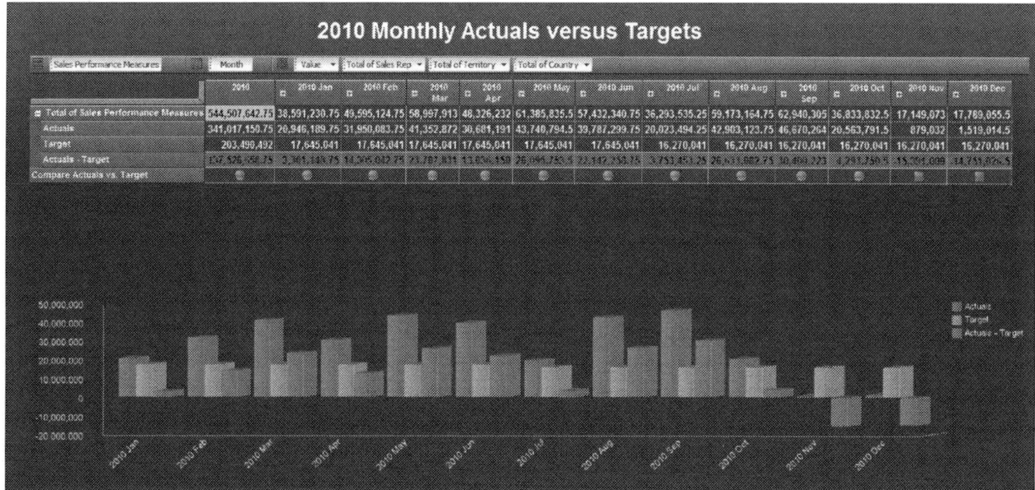

Sales analysis leads to many questions that may change strategy across organizations. Scenarios such as the cost of products being too high, might have an impact on the sales, or poor sales performance can be improved by incentivizing employees with higher benefits to "push" for more sales, especially on new products.

Cognos Insight has proven to point out the "pain points" faced during a similar situation in 2010, which it has captured and analyzed to come up with results. These results will be presented to the client to enable faster decision making using rich visual dashboards.

Finance and price strategy

In *Chapter 1, The New-age Analytics and IBM Cognos Insight*, we learned how companies that do not leverage analytics and go with their gut feelings instead do not tend to make it as top performers in the industry. In some cases, even today, planning and decision-making takes place without factual data analysis. IBM Cognos Insight provides scenario planning capabilities as one of its features that enable planning and forecasting. This technique creates alternate business scenarios to better prepare organizations in solving business-related queries across all the domains.

PointScore is going to leverage this technique in addressing a pricing strategy for the new products being introduced in a market that is not new to its client's competitors. Given the situational awareness, three pricing strategy types have been carefully chosen and are going to be analyzed further using Cognos Insight. The pricing options' objectives are to deliver breakthrough impact into the market, maintain estimated revenue (from previous analysis), and continue upward profit generation over the lifetime of the products. Advanced analysis using Cognos Insight should help achieve these goals.

The selected pricing methods are as follows:

- **Penetration pricing**: As the name suggests, this pricing technique is used for entering a new market and has been selected as one of the options given the launch of new product types

- **Cost plus pricing**: This method is used to maximize profits and is calculated by increasing production until marginal revenue matches marginal costs further determined by the demand

- **Market-oriented pricing**: This pricing option uses prior research efforts to price products, based on consumer feedback, market trends, and other variables that drive the business domain

Financial analysis and pricing strategy should answer some of the following questions and others such as the following:

- Which price model will best suite this product and our organization?

- What should the selling price be based upon competition and consumer spending capacity?

- Will the product be profitable when developed and marketed to the customer?

- What will be the estimated growth rate with a new product?

- How will the product be produced most cost effectively?

PointScore R&D department has researched an average amount of $50.00 per product to be the market retail price of similar products from competitors. We will use this amount to further our analysis.

The following instructions will help build a Product Pricing analysis using Cognos Insight. At the end of these instructions is the final output file as seen in the next screenshot:

1. Double-click on Cognos Insight to start a new workspace.

2. Create a new **Crosstab** from the **Insert** menu.

3. Rename the dimension **A** to **Product Type**.

4. Add a data element called **3-D Gaming**.

5. Rename dimension **B** to **PS Measures** with elements **Production Cost** and **Revenue**.

6. Create a new dimension called **Pricing Strategy** with elements **Penetrating Price, Cost Plus Price**, and **Market-Oriented Price**.

7. Right-click on **Revenue** and **Production Cost**, and select **Calculate**.

8. Create a calculation to show **Profit Revenue-Production Cost**.

From the outcome of the marketing analysis, PointScore was able to determine the production cost for the new products to be at $450 million. Its revenue is predicted to be $540 million.

Hence the analysis reveals that the profit should amount to $90 million.

1. Create a new **Calculation** that divides **Production Cost** by **$50**.

2. Rename this calculation to be **Number of Units**. This calculation reveals 90 million units have to be sold to generate the numbers from the marketing research and analysis.

3. Resize the widget.

4. Drag and drop the existing cube to create a new cube.

5. Reorient the crosstab to show the **Pricing Strategy** dimension as rows and **PS Measures** as columns.

6. Right-click on the columns to create a new column called **Price per Unit**.

7. Right-click on the cell values of both **Production Cost** and **Revenue**. This will hold the costs and allow for the *what-if* scenario. This will help us determine the number of copies to be sold or calculate the pricing options per price strategy method type.

8. Create a new calculation by dividing the **Production Cost** by **Price per Unit**. Apply values to the empty cells to adjust the *what-if* situation in calculating the number of units needed to be sold.

9. Add an appropriate text title.

10. Add descriptive text items next to each crosstab.

11. Lock all the widgets.

As seen in the following screenshot, the three pricing options display the number of units to sell in order to maintain the profits generated from the market research by PointScore.

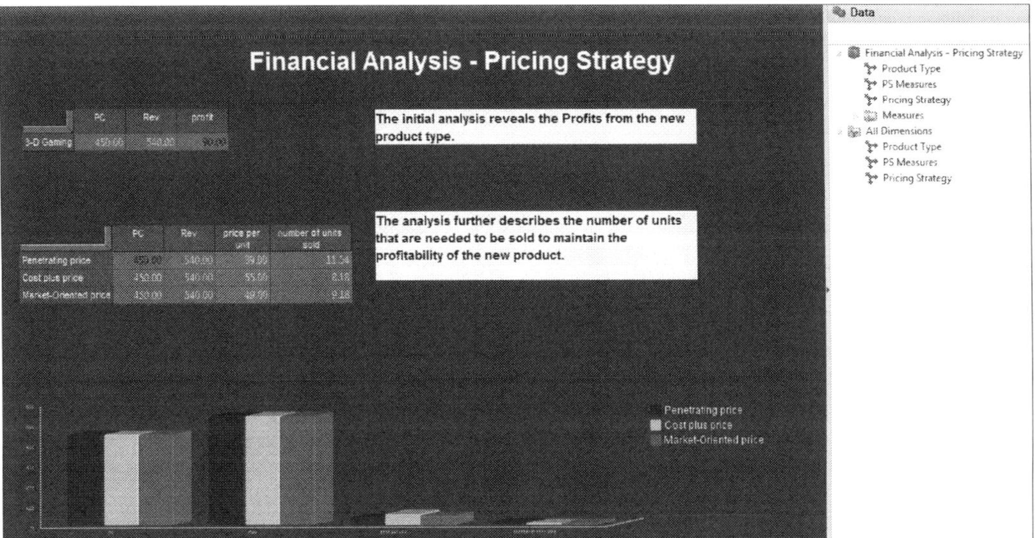

Summary

This chapter used the OLAP concepts and features of IBM Cognos Insight from the previous chapters to create business scenarios for marketing, sales, and finance departments. Building multiple workspaces for different departments shows the flexibility of Cognos Insight to build the dashboard style analysis quickly and effectively. Much more can be derived from the analysis performed by PointScore for its clients and further analyses are left for the readers imagination and business experience.

Building the various workspaces, the analysis revealed that the selling strategy from economic conditions, regions, and other customer demographics. Advertising costs and the effect on the revenue of the new products were displayed using just a few dashboards, built in minutes. Finally, a pricing strategy from three different options were presented to PointScore's client, which will be utilized to promote and develop the new products. The new products are to be targeted towards their existing and new customer base.

The next and the final chapter is going to take the analyses from Cognos Insight and present it using Cognos Business Intelligence. *Chapter 5, Enterprise Collaboration* will focus on sharing the Cognos Insight workspaces with larger user groups by publishing the analysis into IBM Cognos Business Intelligence. The collaborated analysis will then tie in all departments together to maximize productivity and display the same data across the entire organization.

Enterprise Collaboration

In *Chapter 1, The New-age Analytics and IBM Cognos Insight*, we learned the importance of collaborative efforts in analytics for modern business. In 2012, a global study was conducted jointly by IBM's Institute of Business Value (IBV) and **MIT Sloan Management Review**. This study, which included 1700 CEOs globally, reinforced the fact that one of the top objectives within their organizations was sharing and collaboration.

IBM Cognos Insight, the desktop analysis application, provides collaborative features that allow the users to launch development efforts via IBMs Cognos Business Intelligence, Cognos Express, and Performance Management enterprise platforms. We shall visit these as a part of the case study from *Chapter 4, Strategic Decision Making Using IBM Cognos Insight*, by the fictitious company called PointScore.

Having completed its marketing, sales, and price strategy analysis, PointScore is now ready to demonstrate its research and analysis efforts to its client. Using IBM Cognos Insight, PointScore has three available options. All of these will leverage the Cognos Suite of products that its client has been using and is familiar with. Each of these options can be used to share the information with a larger audience within the organization.

Launching workspace files to clients

The following are the three options available for PointScore, as they take Cognos Insight workspace files and launch it to their clients Cognos environment. These options are available in Cognos Insight under the **Actions** menu.

- **Share**: Navigate to **Actions | Share**, as shown in the following screenshot. This method will publish the Cognos Insight workspaces directly into Cognos Business Intelligence. Follow the wizard to share the workspace.

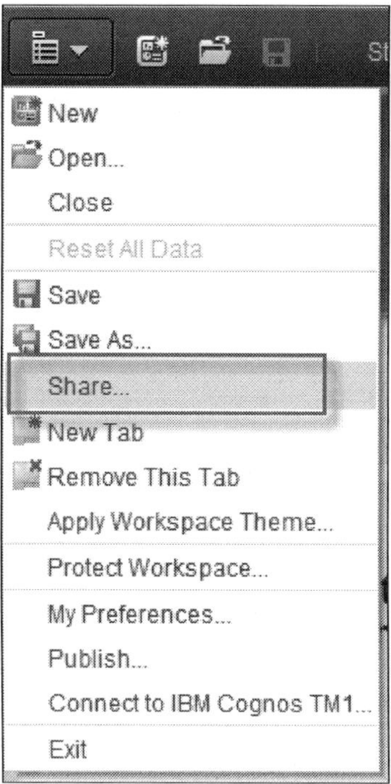

The next image shows the wizard in the process of sharing the workspace files. Use this window to input the Cognos BI URL, login credentials, and the location to publish Cognos Insight:

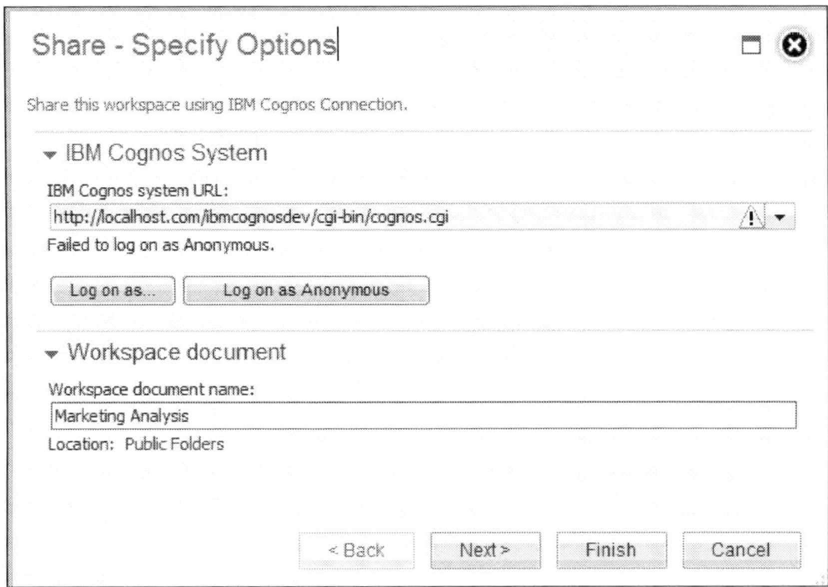

This will take each of the Cognos Insight workspaces and deploy them as is using the wizard into the Cognos Business Intelligence web portal, **Cognos Connection**. Each Cognos Insight workspace (`.cdd` file) will be placed in the Cognos Connection portal location specified in the wizard, as shown in the following screenshot:

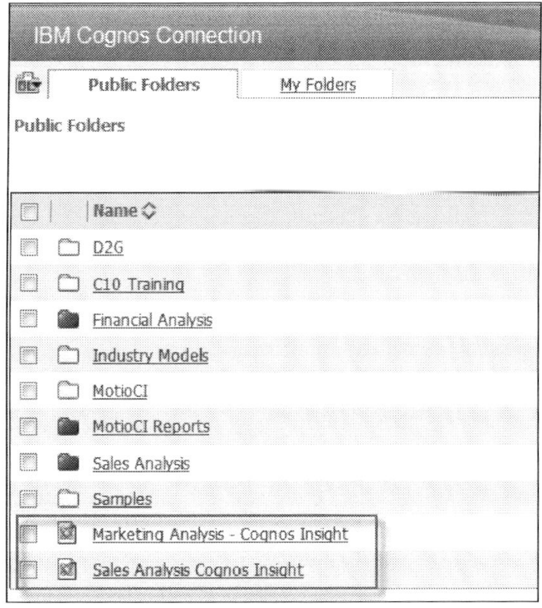

These individual workspaces can now be accessed by anyone that has the appropriate access permissions to download and view the Cognos Insight workspaces.

For those users who do not have IBM Cognos Insight installed on their local computers, a provision install follows when the users click on the Cognos Insight workspace in Cognos Connection. Users can then download the CDD files on their local computers.

- **Publish**: This option will publish Cognos Insight workspaces to the IBM Cognos Application portal. The data belonging to each workspace is stored on an IBM TM1 server to which Cognos Insight connects. This setup can be used to govern and provide access security to the workspaces. This typically should be governed by the IT departments as a centralized hub for all the Cognos Insight workspaces that will be published to the enterprise servers.

As shown in the following screenshot, under the **Action** menu, click on **Publish**.

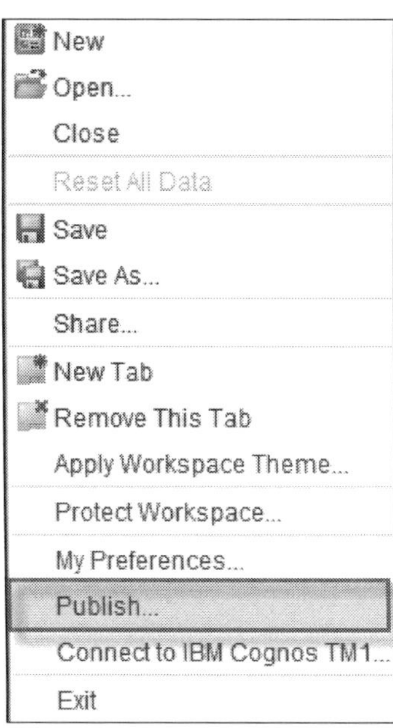

This is followed by a window displaying the **Publish** and **Publish and Distribute** options, as seen in the following screenshot:

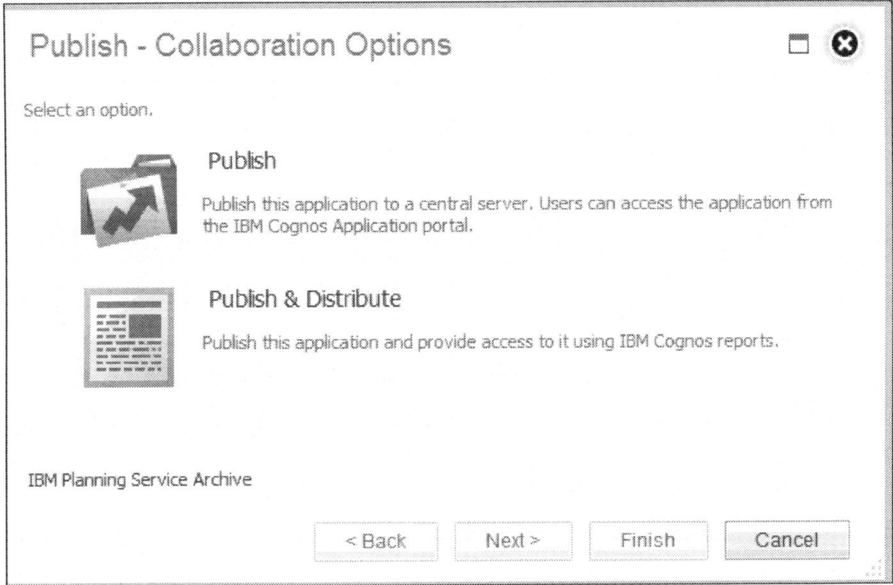

The **Publish** option requires a link to the IBM TM1 server. Follow the instructions in the wizard to publish the Cognos Insight file into the Cognos Application portal.

In the **Publish** wizard, as seen in the following screenshot, select an option for the **Use a dimension to control access to data** field. This selection will centralize security, based on the items specified in the dimension. In this case, customer data elements in the **Customer** dimension will drive the security specifications.

If unchecked, a central application type will be created, which is typically shared by a smaller group of users who share the tasks of planning and data analysis.

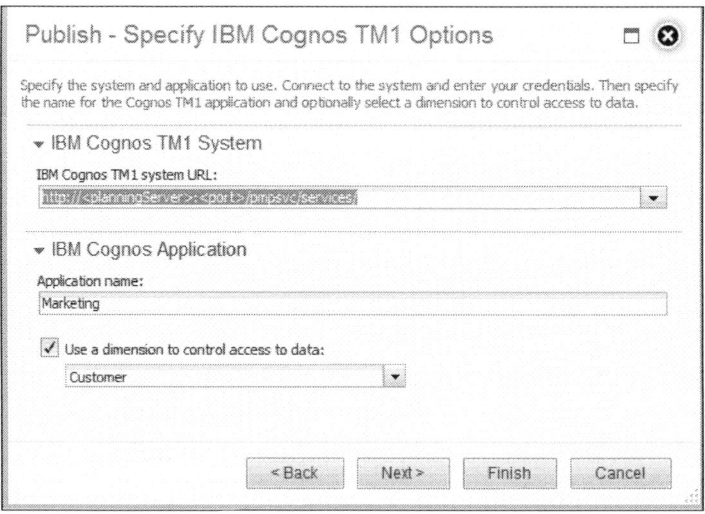

As seen in the following image, a new application is created for each of the Cognos Insight workspaces that have successfully been published to the Cognos Application Portal:

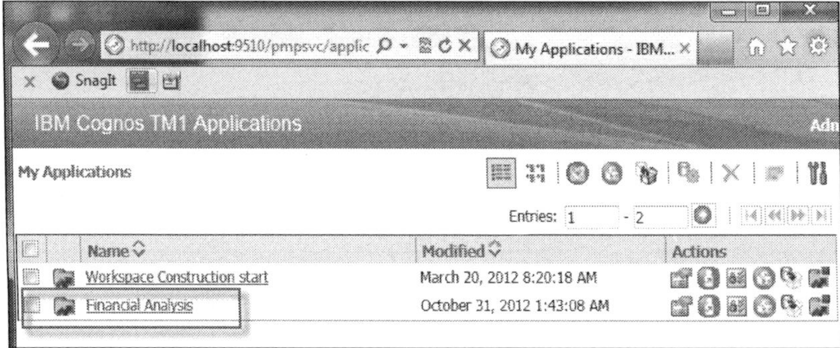

By clicking on each application, user permissions and the amount of data they can view or contribute to in their plans can be controlled, as seen in the following screenshot:

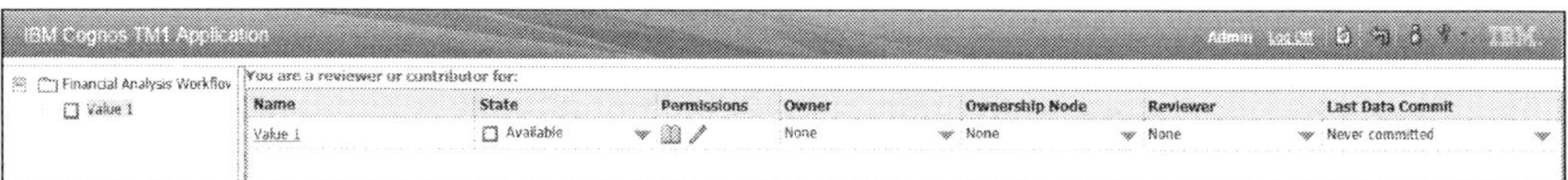

The **Publish** option provides a centralized approach, where administrative governance can be applied by the responsible departments or employees. Secured data resides on the TM1 server to keep a controlled access on the users contributing to the enterprise server. In the disconnected mode, the users can continue to contribute to their plans and sync up data changes to the centralized server, once back online.

- **Publish and Distribute**: The **Publish and Distribute** option converts the Cognos Insight workspaces into Cognos BI reports. Using the wizard, input the TM1 server information and Cognos BI web portal information. A data source is created in Cognos Connection and a Cognos package is published into the desired location. This package contains Cognos BI reports, created from Cognos Insight widgets that can be accessed using Cognos reporting studios.

As seen in the following screenshot, the Financial Analysis Cognos Insight workspace has been published into the Cognos BI and IBM TM1 environments:

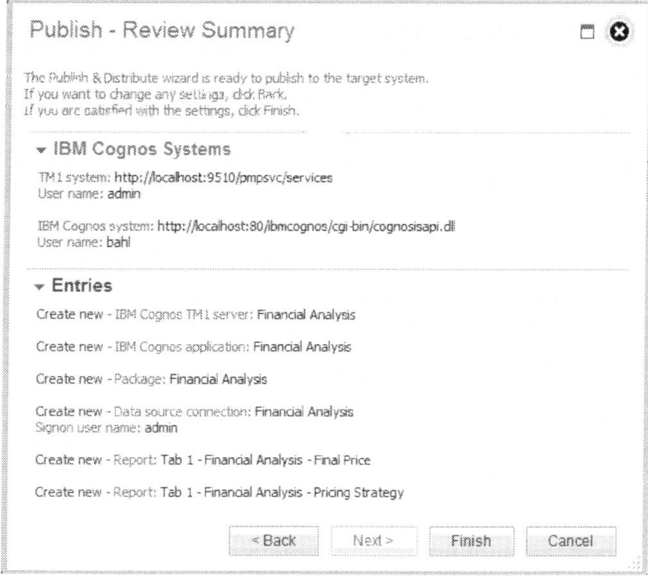

The summary page in the wizard verifies the creation of the following items:

- A new TM1 server
- A new application in the Cognos Application portal
- A new Cognos BI package
- A new Cognos BI data source
- New Report Studio reports for each widget on the Cognos Insight workspace

To verify if the **Publish and Distribute** created these objects, begin by looking into Cognos Connection. The following image shows the Administration Studio and the newly-created data source connection:

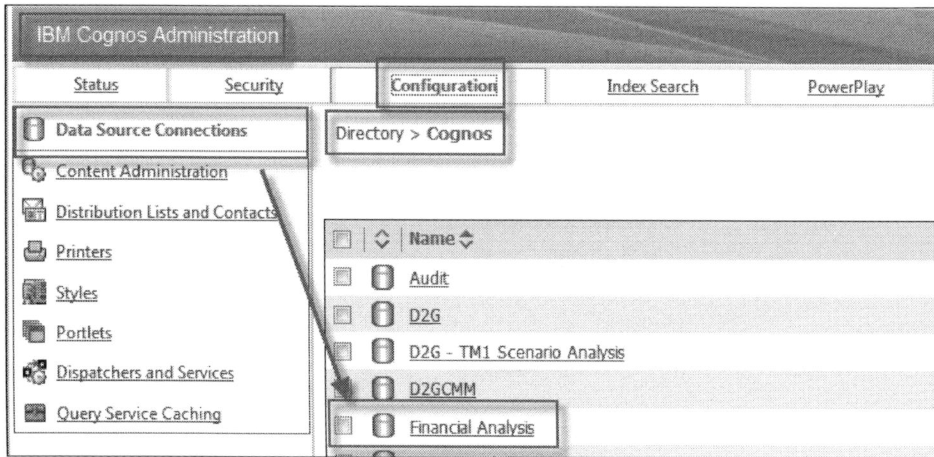

Next, the Cognos package will exist in the **Public Folders**, as seen in the following screenshot:

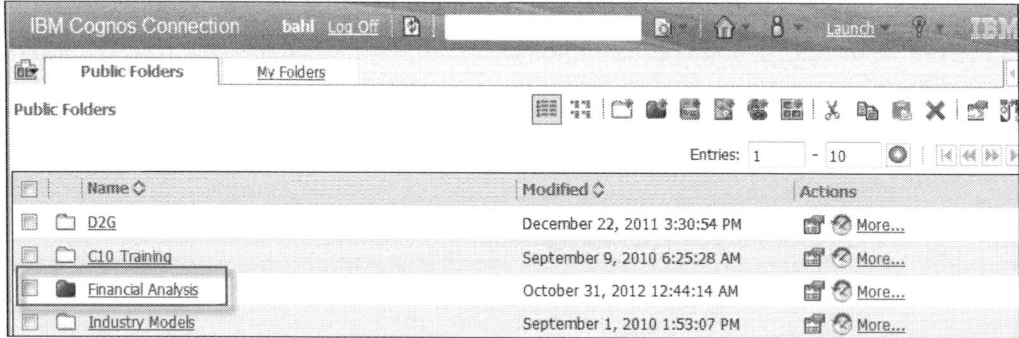

Click on the **Finance Package** option. This will display the newly-created Cognos Report Studio reports. This is a huge advantage in using Cognos Insight and the **Publish and Distribute** mode—the widgets within the Cognos Insight workspaces are converted into reports in Cognos BI, as seen in the following screenshot:

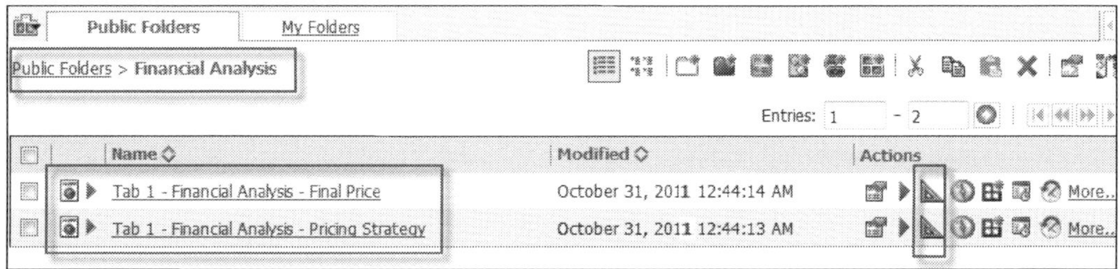

Leveraging IBM Cognos Insight collaboration and sharing

PointScore decides to use the third option—**Publish and Distribute**—to share its analysis with the client leveraging their existing Cognos BI and TM1 environments. PointScore uses the **Publish and Distribute** wizard to input their client's web links for both, TM1 and Cognos BI. The data and reports now reside in the client's environment.

PointScore is going to provide a demonstration to its clients on its findings, using Cognos Business Insight (renamed to **Cognos Workspace** in BI version 10.2). This web studio makes building dashboards easier for the business user by dragging and dropping the existing BI content onto a canvas.

As seen in the following screenshot, Cognos Insight dashboards have seamlessly been integrated with the company's existing BI content, and a quick dashboard for business users has been created in Cognos Business Insight.

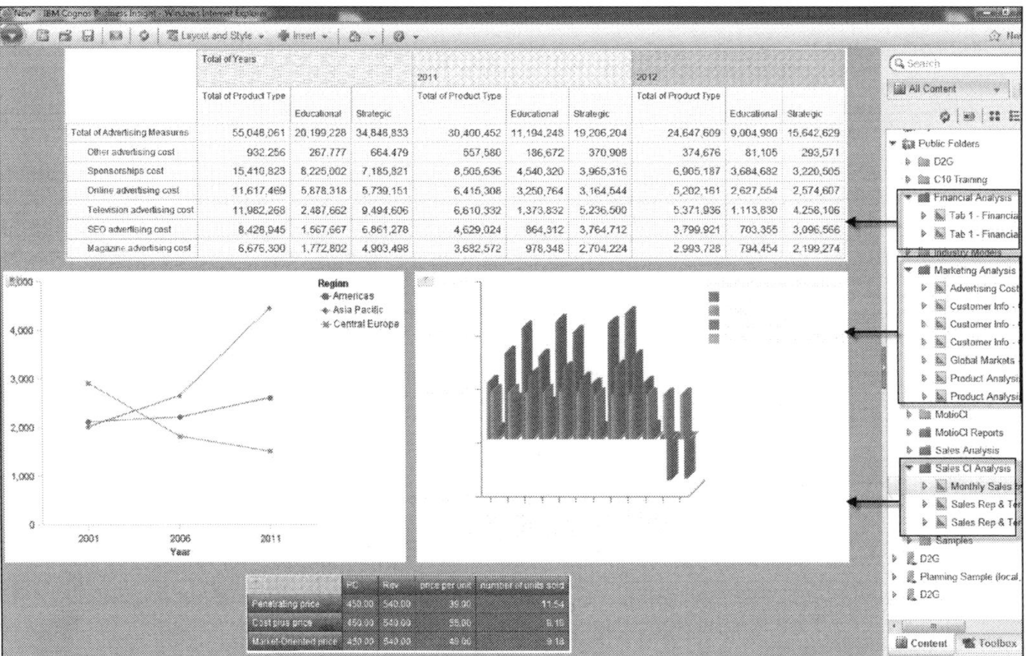

Now that the Cognos Insight data files have been published into the Cognos BI system, the client can now perform their own analysis. This newly-imported data asset can be worked on as a collaborative effort. Department heads assign plans or segments of plans to analysts and contributors to allow the *what-if* analysis. These plans are then submitted for approvals, and are either accepted or rejected. When changes are accepted and saved to the TM1 server, a lockdown takes place until the particular plan is rejected. There are two types of collaboration methods, which are as follows:

- **Distributed mode**: As the name suggests, distributed mode is used when the user base contributing to plans is large. Ownership of plans or portions of plans are allowed only at the lowest level (leaf level). As there are numerous resources working on portions of the same plan, an unlimited number of data changes can be made. This is because they are stored on local machines, until those changes are committed to and submitted. Thereafter, the changes are sent to the TM1 server from where the entire user base can view the newly-updated plans.

- **Connected mode**: For the situations where the data is updated frequently and the size of the data is very large, the connected mode is preferred. Data is saved directly to the server and not locally; but the ownership can be taken from any level.

From researching and performing in-house analysis using IBM Cognos Insight, PointScore leveraged its client's IBM Business Analytics applications to seamlessly publish Cognos Insight to an enterprise level Business Intelligence environment. This methodology minimized the re-work efforts, reduced development periods, and combined the functionalities of these applications so that the client could share and collaborate data to a larger audience. The client also uses Motio CI's capabilities as a version control, stress test and impact analysis product. This impressive product integrates into Cognos BI and enhances the clients environment.

This newly published data can also be consumed using Cognos BI Mobile, which provides a rich, interactive, and intuitive experience on mobile devices such as smart phones and tablets. Users of IBM Cognos Mobile technology can benefit from features such as prompt selections, drilling up and down, and cell highlights to use their Cognos reports and dashboards to answer business-related questions on the go.

Summary

This chapter discussed the various methods of publishing Cognos Insight into Cognos BI and TM1 products. The sharing and collaboration functionality within Cognos Insight puts tremendous power into the desktop application. Be it contributing to offline/online plans or consuming BI reports via mobile technology, Cognos Insight—collaborated with larger audiences using menu-driven options—quickly turned desktop analysis into enterprise-wide collaborative efforts.

Though technical, this book is written for a non-technical audience as well. IBM Cognos Insight is a product that has its roots embedded in Business Intelligence and its foundation is built upon Performance Management solutions. This book provides the readers with Business Analytics techniques and discusses the technical aspects of the product, describing its features and benefits.

The goal of writing this book was to make you feel confident about the product and to use the book as a reference guide. As *Chapter 3, Usability of Cognos Insight* provides screenshots of every feature, *Chapter 4, Strategic Decision Making Using IBM Cognos Insight*, is meant to expand on your creativity and broaden the scope of your vision to align with each individual's experiences and business background, so that the reader can build better analysis and workspaces using Cognos Insight.

The final chapter focuses on the strengths of the product, which is to share and collaborate the development efforts into an existing IBM Cognos BI, Cognos Express, or TM1 environment. This sharing is possible because of the tight integration among all the products under the IBM Business Analytics umbrella.

After reading this book, you should be able to tackle Business Analytics implementations from a bottom-up and a cross-functional approach and leverage the sharing capability to reach an end goal of spreading the value of Business Analytics throughout their organizations.

References

The following sources will be quite valuable to you:

- `www.ibm.com` (IBM Software | Products | Business Analytics)
- IBM IBV *Analytics: The new path to value*
- *IBM Journal of Research and Development Vol 2 Number 4, Oct 1958*
- *IBM 2011 Tech Trends Report*
- `www.wimbledon.com` (IBM Slamtracker)
- *Business Intelligence Strategy: A Practical Guide for Achieving BI Excellence, John Boyer, Bill Frank, Brian Green, Tracy Harris,* and *Kay Van De Vanter, MC Press Online, LLC*
- *The Performance Manager: Proven Strategies for Turning Information into Higher Business Performance, Roland Mosimann, Patrick Mosimann,* and *Meg Dussault, Cognos Press*
- Wikipedia – Pricing Strategy (`http://en.wikipedia.org/wiki/Pricing_strategies`)
- *Performance Dashboards and Analysis for Value Creation, Jack Alexander, John Wiley & Sons, Inc.*
- `www.analyticszone.com`
- *IBM Cognos Insight User Guide*
- IBM Cognos Insight Supported Environments (`http://www-01.ibm.com/support/docview.wss?uid=swg27025127`)

Index

Thank you for buying
IBM Cognos Insight

About Packt Publishing

Packt, pronounced 'packed', published its first book "Mastering phpMyAdmin for Effective MySQL Management" in April 2004 and subsequently continued to specialize in publishing highly focused books on specific technologies and solutions.

Our books and publications share the experiences of your fellow IT professionals in adapting and customizing today's systems, applications, and frameworks. Our solution based books give you the knowledge and power to customize the software and technologies you're using to get the job done. Packt books are more specific and less general than the IT books you have seen in the past. Our unique business model allows us to bring you more focused information, giving you more of what you need to know, and less of what you don't.

Packt is a modern, yet unique publishing company, which focuses on producing quality, cutting-edge books for communities of developers, administrators, and newbies alike. For more information, please visit our website: www.packtpub.com.

About Packt Enterprise

In 2010, Packt launched two new brands, Packt Enterprise and Packt Open Source, in order to continue its focus on specialization. This book is part of the Packt Enterprise brand, home to books published on enterprise software – software created by major vendors, including (but not limited to) IBM, Microsoft and Oracle, often for use in other corporations. Its titles will offer information relevant to a range of users of this software, including administrators, developers, architects, and end users.

Writing for Packt

We welcome all inquiries from people who are interested in authoring. Book proposals should be sent to author@packtpub.com. If your book idea is still at an early stage and you would like to discuss it first before writing a formal book proposal, contact us; one of our commissioning editors will get in touch with you.

We're not just looking for published authors; if you have strong technical skills but no writing experience, our experienced editors can help you develop a writing career, or simply get some additional reward for your expertise.

IBM Cognos 10 Business Intelligence

ISBN: 978-1-84968-356-2   Paperback: 450 pages

A practical approach to all things IBM Cognos 10 Business Intelligence.

1. Learn how to better administer your IBM Cognos 10 environment in order to improve productivity and efficiency.

2. Empower your business with the latest Business Intelligence (BI) tools.

3. Discover advanced tools and knowledge that can greatly improve daily tasks and analysis.

4. Explore the new interfaces of IBM Cognos 10.

IBM Cognos Business Intelligence 10.1 Dashboarding Cookbook

ISBN: 978-1-84968-582-5   Paperback: 206 pages

Working with dashboards in IBM Cognos BI 10.1 Design, distribute, and collaborate

1. Exploring and interacting with IBM Cognos Business Insight and Business Insight Advanced

2. Creating dashboards in IBM Cognos Business Insight and Business Insight Advanced

3. Sharing and Collaborating on Dashboards using portlets

4. Best practices related to Dashboards in Cognos 10.1

Please check **www.PacktPub.com** for information on our titles

IBM Cognos 8 Planning

ISBN: 978-1-84719-684-2   Paperback: 424 pages

A practical guide to developing and deploying planning models for your enterprise

1. Build and deploy effective planning models using Cognos 8 Planning

2. Filled with ideas and techniques for designing planning models

3. Ample screenshots and clear explanations to facilitate learning

4. Written for first-time developers focusing on what is important to the beginner

IBM Cognos TM1 Cookbook

ISBN: 978-1-84968-210-7   Paperback: 490 pages

Build real world planning, budgeting, and forecasting solutions with a collection of over 60 simple but incredibly effective recipes

1. A comprehensive developer's guide for planning, building, and managing practical applications with IBM TM1

2. No prior knowledge of TM1 expected

3. Complete coverage of all the important aspects of IBM TM1 in carefully planned step-by-step practical demos

Please check **www.PacktPub.com** for information on our titles